D1321681

Overcoming
Indecisiveness

The Eight Stages of
Effective Decision-making

Books by Theodore Isaac Rubin

Autobiography

Emergency Room Diary
Shrink
Reflections in a Goldfish Tank
Through My Own Eyes

Fiction

Jordi
Lisa and David
In the Life
Sweet Daddy
Cat
Platzo and the Mexican Pony Rider
The 29th Summer
Coming Out

Nonfiction

The Thin Book by a Formerly Fat Psychiatrist
The Winner's Note Book
The Angry Book
Dr Rubin, Please Make Me Happy
Compassion and Self-Hate
Understanding Your Man [with David Berliner]
Love Me Love My Fool
Forever Thin
Alive and Fat and Thinning in America
Reconciliations
One to One
Not to Worry [with Eleanor Rubin]
Overcoming Indecisiveness

Overcoming Indecisiveness

The Eight Stages of Effective Decision-making

Dr Theodore Isaac Rubin

CEDAR

First published in the USA 1985
by Harper & Row Publishers, New York

First published in Great Britain 1990 by Cedar
an imprint of Mandarin
Michelin House, 81 Fulham Road, London SW3 6RB
Reprinted 1990

Mandarin is an imprint of the Octopus Publishing Group

A CIP catalogue record for this book
is available from the British Library

Hardback ISBN 0 434 65534 1
Paperback ISBN 0 434 11165 1

Printed in Great Britain
by Cox and Wyman Ltd, Reading, Berks.

To Ellie Rubin,
who knew how to make them right from the start

Multitudes, multitudes in the valley of decision . . .

Joel 3:14

Once a decision was made,
I did not worry about it afterward.

Harry S Truman

Contents

III

Priorities: Applying Who We Really Are to the Decisions We Make   79

Contents .... *xi*

VII

Preface

*B*eing able to make decisions is an enormous privilege.

There is little as life-enhancing, as constructive to success in all areas, and as important to happiness as the ability to make decisions.

Decisions put us in charge of our own lives. Every time we make a real decision, we find out who we really are, because we make use of our own priorities and values.

On the other hand, difficulty with decisions complicates all aspects of our lives. It blocks emotional growth and development, leads to multiple failures—especially in relationships—and contributes to the repression of feelings, sowing the seeds of poor health.

Indecision and malignant ambivalence are the stuff of powerlessness, frustration, envy, rage, bitterness, cynicism and chronic hopelessness.

There are many people who have great difficulty making decisions; some cannot make decisions at all. But however impeded or healthy, no free adult can avoid decision-making. And fortunately, nearly everyone can improve his or her decision-making ability.

That is what this book is all about: understanding and solving problems, making real and free decisions in all areas of life—and in a better way. The basic principles of real, successful decision-making apply to all types of decisions: business or personal, straightforward or complex, trivial or momentous.

I am intersted in helping you achieve the tremendous power good decision-makers have in living happy and productive lives.

In my relationships with people, both professional and otherwise, I have consistently been struck by the great difficulty so many of us have making decisions. One of the great satisfadtions in the practice of psychoanalytic psychotherapy is the relief felt by patients and the effectiveness of their efforts in all aspects of their lives when they learn to recognize this problem and deal with it successfully.

It is my hope that in reading this book you will derive great relief and satisfaction from learning more about the decision process and about yourself.

THEODORE ISAAC RUBIN

New York
June 1984

Acknowledgements

*S*pecial thanks to Dona Munker, consulting editor, whose initiative, enthusiasm, and understanding of the subject were vital in bringing this book about; and to Sallie Coolidge of Harper & Row, Inc., for her superb editing and continuing faith.

Who This Book Is For

Abdicators
Administrators
Artists
Brides
Businessmen
and
Businesswomen
Car Buyers
Counselors
Dieters
Doctors
Editors
Engineers
Executives
Fishermen
Fund-raisers
Hedonists
Hermits
House-hunters
Impulse-chasers
Ironmongers

Lawyers
Lovers
Managers
Moralists
Parents
Policemen
Policymakers
Procrastinators
Romantics
Sailors
Smokers
Social Workers
Students
Teachers
Tennis Players
Wallflowers
Wishful Thinkers
Wives
Husbands
Men
Women

I feel it is for anyone who has ever had trouble making up his or her mind

I

Real Decisions

Abdication and Making Real Decisions

It is very important that we understand the difference between abdication and real decisions. They represent different modes of behavior and sometimes whole different ways of life.

In abdication, we either resign completely from the decision-making process or so pervert the process as to almost negate it. Thus, we neglect and ignore, at least to some degree, most aspects of our true selves. In making real decisions, perhaps more than in any process in life, we involve ourselves fully.

The connections real decisions have to frustration and failure and to success and happiness will become apparent in this section.

Decision Ownership!

*W*hen I was a midshipman in office training school, I had a brilliant and interesting commanding officer. All of us felt he deserved to be an admiral in charge of a fleet.

Captain Brown lectured us again and again on the importance of being able to give an order. He pointed out that orders were based on decisions. Some required time, and sometimes there *was* plenty of time for research, choice and planning. But there were "command decisions" which, in the heat of sea battles, had to be translated into orders instantaneously.

He repeatedly impressed us with the fact that as line officers we had to make decisions *our very own* and accept responsibility for their outcome. Furthermore, a man who could not give an order, who would not accept responsibility, who would not risk a mistake for whatever reason—whether perfectionism, poor self-esteem or vanity—must not be in any command position. He pointed out that at sea, apathy, indecision, inhibition and paralysis could result not in mere mistakes but in catastrophic tragedies.

"Decide and order," he told us. To practice, each of us "gave orders" to marching platoons, sailboat crews, docking crews, shore battery drill crews. Our mistakes became fewer. Decisions and orders became easier. We also made mistakes and corrected them, increasing our flexibility, our morale, and our fund of knowledge.

Real decisions do that: They integrate and unify various aspects of ourselves, translating theory into action. They increase self-esteem. Decision power increases geometrically, because the very act of decision-making breaks through inhibition and paralysis.

Conversely, prolonged apathy, indecision, paralysis and inhibition can result not just in mistakes but in disaster.

The Other System

The world is divided unequally between decision-makers and abdicators.

The majority of us tend to be abdicators. At least to some degree, we forgo our freedom to make decisions. If we abdicate a great deal, it will be reflected by chronic failure. Success as a way of life is directly proportional to the willingness to make decisions.

Most of us are not at all aware of how we abdicate. We wait for things to happen instead of making them happen. We doubt or criticize decisions we were committed to, make so-called decisions out of panic or let others decide for us. We turn away from goals we know we could achieve and want to achieve.

Enormous unhappiness, multiple failures in all areas of life, opportunities lost, deep frustrations, endless procrastination and abiding hopelessness are some of the results of abdication. Unfortunately, we rarely connect these symptoms with their cause. In fact, even the most chronic abdicators are seldom aware of their infirmity. I have known people virtually paralyzed by indecision who did not know they had any difficulty at all making decisions. This is in part because they did not know what constitutes making a real decision.

Let me give you some common symptoms of abdication.

Joe sits in a restaurant, stares at a menu and waits until his wife orders. He then orders whatever she does. His selection does not reflect his own taste, choice or decision. Later in the evening, he feels that his wife has bullied him. He is irritated with her and with himself.

Sally is lonely. She is waiting for that special person to come along. But she meets few people because she works all day and then goes directly home. She thinks of going places where there are people, but does not translate the thought into decisive action. She is quite attractive, though few people see her. She hopes that the right person will materialize; somehow, someday, she is almost sure he will. She continues to be a wallflower in life, spending nearly all her time in the office or at home—isolated.

Rex is a middle-level administrator in a big city agency responsible for the purchase of extremely expensive computer equipment. He works day and night assembling bids and data from different companies to determine the best purchase for the department's money. But something always keeps him from making a choice until he absolutely has to make it. "I need the pressure of a deadline," he says. "It helps me think and I can make a better decision that way." When the deadline approaches, he feels panicky and ends up recommending whichever company he knows the most about. He often feels guilty, depressed and unhappy—as well as fearful that someday he'll make one expensive mistake too many and lose his job. But, "I just trust to luck," he says, "and figure that things will take care of themselves.'

John, a high-level political policymaker in Washington, talks about changing jobs. His dissatisfaction with his work goes back many years. It is his main topic of conversation. He is fifty years old. "Nothing has happened," he complains. He does nothing to change jobs and he ignores or puts off pressing policy decisions because "it's all pointless anyway." He is unhappy and believes his friends are bored with him. He is especially angry at those who have "moved on" to positions he considers more interesting. "Some people are lucky," he says. He feels that he is paralyzed, but is unable to contemplate changing careers. He does not know why. He never has known why. The paralysis seems to have a life of its own.

Paula thinks she wants to win her club's tennis championship. But then, in the middle of the game, she becomes self-conscious. "It's as if there are two of me—one playing and one watching me play and wondering if I really want this for myself." At that point, her game "comes apart" and she loses.

These are real examples and they are not at all unusual. They are so commonplace that we usually don't recognize them for what they are—an inability to make and carry out decisions that are our very own.

"Something is Missing"

*T*hose of us who chronically abdicate the decision process feel that something is missing from life. A more accurate way to describe the problem would be to say that "some*one* is missing."

Abdicators are missing from giving direction, input and development to their lives. *They* are missing!

When good things do happen, it seems not to be truly theirs or of their making. Therefore their accomplishments do not add to self-esteem, identity or a feeling of substantiality. Envy of people who "have more luck" often generates hostile feelings and disturbed, frustrating relationships.

The accomplishments of abdicators are invariably limited. The simple fact is that success in any area of life requires full participation and commitment to a choice.

Joe can't take responsibility for ordering food. In actuality, Joe probably lost touch with what tastes good to him some time ago. In so doing he dulled his tastes, his proclivities, his judgment and his spontaneity. I am certain that this small 'symptom' is evidence of many other areas where Joe has abdicated decision-making.

Sally can't take responsibility for making the decision to go out and meet people. She can't bring herself to participate fully in her own life. Waiting for the right person to "happen" to her practically guarantees that she never will.

Rex can't accept responsibility for a fully thought out decision about what computers to recommend. I have no doubt that there are many other areas of life in which he leaves the decision up to "fate" and pays the price of guilt, depression and the sense that his life is not really his own.

John cannot bring himself to decide to risk a change of careers. Instead, he bitterly blames "getting left behind" on fate and takes out his anger on those who have been "luckier." He is stultified, paralyzed to the point where he lacks even the spontaneity needed to investigate himself.

Paula loses in tennis because she is not a full participant. How can she be? She isn't really sure how important winning the club championship is to her. In fact, Paula is not fully dedicated to *winning* in any area of life. She wants the fruits of victory but she fears the exposure and vulnerability of complete participation. Therefore only half of Paula plays; the other half not only is missing from the game but also questions the wisdom of her participation, and ultimately wrecks her chances of winning.

Whenever we abdicate, large areas of ourselves go unemployed and "atrophy"—they become unavailable to us and cannot be felt, reached or used. This produces anxiety and a sense of inner deadness and emptiness. Moreover, each succeeding abdication adds to the clash of inner conflicting forces and, despite noisy, clamorous distractions, makes us feel dull, depressed and fatigued.

But full commitment and acceptance of our decisions as our own have just the opposite effect. They keep us feeling alive, vital, in touch with our tastes and values. This is so because every time we make a real decision, we tap and make use of our whole selves—tastes, values, priorities, judgment ability and energy—in integrated action.

Real Decisions

*W*hat is a "real" decision?

In the simplest, most basic terms, a real decision is a *free, unconditional, total and personal commitment* to a choice or option, or a group of them.

Psychoanalysts use the term "emotional investment." For me, emotional investment means feeling strongly and caring enough to invest time, energy, thought, talent and assets in the issue and its outcome.

In real decision-making, nothing is held back. This means our feelings as well as our logic, so that we are *committed* to the choice we have made.

A logical set of questions at this point is: Can I change my mind? If I change my mind, is this evidence that the decision was not a real one?

Of course you can change your mind. Healthy flexibility is desirable in life and is characteristic of decision-makers. To be paralyzed by indecision is a sign of abdication. By the same token, compulsively going up and back and sideways indicates, not freedom, but a deadlock in a pattern of indecision—what I call pseudodecision.

A healthy change of mind does not mean jumping from one position to another, satisfying autonomous fragments of the self, either to avoid a decision or to fulfill all the options. Real and healthy changes of mind can always occur after real decisions have been made, when you are unified about your choice and decide that conditions have altered sufficiently to warrant a change. Such mind-changing is based on reality and occurs in all people who own their decisions. The other type occurs in people who have a long history of chronic indecision.

As I have said, decision constitutes *full commitment to a favored choice.* Decision also constitutes *full commitment to one road only*—the road that leads to the favored choice. If the situation alters, we may, after careful consideration, change our minds. But as long as that reality does not alter, the commitment remains *unconditional.*

The decision you make is *personal*; it is yours alone. That means the center of your life is not in other people's hands. For that reason, real decisions restore, augment and sustain a healthy, positive sense of self; they add to the personal feeling of solidity and increase self-confidence.

The decision is *free*, for it has been reached without inner threat or coercion and without fear of any self-recrimination or reprisal, especially for not complying with others' wishes.

It is *total*, because the whole self is involved—not just a portion—thus facilitating and supporting unconditional commitment.

The *commitment* thus achieved is more than just not looking back. It is a dedication of the full self in which we integrate, unify and mobilize all our assets for the favored choice. This concentration of inner resources has a unifying and therapeutic effect. Above all, commitment smoothly and efficiently translates choices into integrated action and action into goal fulfillment and success.

Remember that decisions—real decisions—make you own more of yourself. My navy captain knew that. He also knew the value of the process of decision-making in the service of any kind of goal completion, in the navy or elsewhere.

Pseudodecisions

*T*he purpose of making pseudodecisions is to avoid real decisions.

Pseudodecisions often look like the real thing.

They are not!

In fact, they always impede real decision-making. Under the guise of being real, they invariably block successful commitment.

Too many people can't understand why they fail again and again when they "make decisions all the time." These are almost invariably long-suffering victims of pseudodecisions which are usually recognizable by their failure to produce successful results.

Of course, no human being is exempt from occasional indecisiveness. However, many people who seem successful to all outward appearances have serious difficulty with commitment, especially in certain areas.

Much suffering and unhappiness in everyday life can result from this unrecognized indecisiveness. I know a wealthy and successful literary agent who has always wanted to write children's books, but she has never been able to get herself started. She has enough experience as a literary professional to know that she has some talent. But whenever she begins to get excited about her ideas and make notes, she suddenly feels "discouraged at all the competition." Though she longs to feel differently so she can begin writing, she is unable to overcome her paralysis.

Paralysis, undermining commitment and avoiding conflicting feelings are all forms of indecision. We may use one or more varities of pseudodecision to avoid decisions; many people combine all of them, and become quite skillful at making them look like real decisions.

Later on, when we discuss blockages, we will come to understand the dynamics of the actual forces that produce pseudodecisions. For pseudodecisions, as synthetic, poor substitutes for real decisions, are the bastard children of blockages to real decisions. But it is important at this point to become acquainted with pseudodecisions, which so often fool the victim into believing that he or she is making real decisions, when actually no such thing is happening. Let me tell you briefly about some of the favorites.

Procrastination

Carol has worked as an editor in a publishing house for twenty years. About eight years ago, it became apparent that she had outgrown her job, and that it was time for her to move up the ladder. She was told, however, that publishing companies, including her own, preferred to appoint upper-level executives from outside the firm. She would be best able to get a promotion, therefore, by moving to another company.

But she procrastinated. Perhaps her company would

recognize her true value after all, she thought. And then, she knew her way around the company she was in. She liked the people she worked with. She decided to wait.

She continued to wait. Finally, in deep frustration—because, truth to tell, after twenty years she was not just overqualified but also bored with the lack of growth and responsibility—she decided to move.

But it was too late. Most companies were suspicious of the fact that she had not made more progress for the length of time she had been in the business; others thought she was too old; still others felt that she was too "imprinted" with the ideas and methodology of the company she had worked with so long. And exacerbating everything, the publishing business was in a state of decline.

Carol's problem, procrastination, was as common as her fate. But the point is that Carol's fate was the one she herself decided on—or rather made a pseudodecision about.

Of course, there are times when waiting to make a decision is appropriate and healthy.

But endless procrastination is often used as a substitute for healthy waiting and represents a pseudodecision. We almost always know when we are dealing with malignant waiting, because (1) the delaying tactic is used repeatedly in issue after issue; (2) for all the waiting, no growth, increased clarification or real change occurs; (3) no healthy conclusion is arrived at; (4) the pseudodecisionmaker, despite a passable appearance of activity, contributes nothing that would bring about real change, but simply "waits for something to turn up." People who use this pseudodecision process a lot are frequently inert to the point of paralysis.

Ambivalence: The Inability to Choose

Ambivalence often goes hand in hand with procrastination, and with "waiting for something to turn up."

We are all ambivalent at times. A large part of maturity is the ability to surrender some desires and to prioritize in order to achieve decisive action. But we often use our mixed feelings as a way of avoiding real choice as we flit from one pseudodecision to another, or as we evade decision entirely because "all the possibilities are so good" or "none of the choices is quite perfect."

Impulse Moves

"Decisions" born of impulse are not decisions at all. They usually backfire into minor or major disasters, depending on the issue. They are nearly always attempts at breaking through profound inertia.

And impulse moves are not real decisions at all because they are the antithesis of free choice. Unlike the real thing, they are always based on anxiety, habit, fear of the unfamiliar, and self-hate.

Letting Someone Else Decide:
Inappropriate Dependency

Most of us have gotten caught up in this one, and many of us get caught frequently. But there are people who have unwittingly traded away large areas of their lives through this form of pseudodecision. In trading the right to make one's own choices and establish one's own opinions for a spurious "peace," one barters away a large part of the self, and identity.

Going Against the Tide

This is another, more subtle, form of dependency. There are people who always decide to do the opposite of what others do, or appear to do. These are compulsive rebels who often fool themselves (and other people too) into thinking that they are independent decision-makers because they always go against the prevailing option or fashion. Of course, they are no such thing: They cannot make a decision until someone else makes it so that they know which road is the opposite one to take. They are just as dependent on others as the more obvious conformer. They, too, lack the self-confidence necessary to tap their own feelings. Their underlying dependency produces great self-hatred, and the false show of rigid rebelliousness is an attempt to avoid this self-hatred by disguising the dependency. Unfortunately, and paradoxically, the self-hatred is perpetuated this way, because the compulsive show of independence is actually just another form of compliance.

Of course, the constructive use of other people's input can be very valuable, as long as we do not allow ourselves to be overwhelmed by superpersuasive people, or talked into ignoring our own feelings and wishes. If we make the decision after a full consideration of our own feelings and priorities as well as other people's input, we are probably making a real decision.

One Foot In and One Foot Out, or Trying to Work All the Options and Having None of Them

Commitment and complete, successful follow-through on the decision you have made are just about synonymous, because follow-through always suggests genuine commitment. Therefore, any decision that leads to having one foot in the room and one foot out the door is not a decision in the first place. Attempting to satisfy all options at the same time without giving up any of them may look like a decision. But it is really a way of avoiding decision.

Looking Back, Foot-Dragging and Wondering What Might Have Been

Looking back or foot-dragging or continuous ruminating about what might have been had another road been taken is always characteristic of pseudodecision-making.

Though the pseudodecider may state that a real decision has been made and may proceed on this belief, compulsive ruminating indicates a fundamental lack of emotional commitment to the decision. Backward glances are attempts to bring other options to the foreground so as to neutralize the decision supposedly made. Moreover, looking back and foot-dragging are usually evidence of an infantile desire and belief that we can have everything we want—that all options can be satisfied at the same time.

We all suffer at least to some extent from the burden of pseudodecisions. The difference between pseudo and real decisions will become more apparent as we go along. The central fact remains that a pseudodecision is self-depleting. The antithesis is true of real decisions. In fact, *every time you make a real decision, you own more of yourself.*

True decision-making produces growth! Real decisions tap our inner resources. They involve us in a healthy struggle that brings a sense of satisfaction and increased self-esteem even in the midst of some very difficult decisions. Real decisions have an inner "binding effect" that gives us a feeling of solid identity. Sometimes a genuine decision can come about quite rapidly, creating an outward appearance of impulsivity—but as you will see when I discuss the actual decision-making process in Chapter 4, in such a case the tapping of resources and the necessary struggle have already been going on unconsciously all along. The signs of real decision are within, not without. Though real decisions produce outward success, it is inner growth, not the out-come of the choice, that points to effective decision-making.

Abdicators and pseudodecision-makers give up the most important psychological freedom that exists—the freedom to make choices and decisions. Some people believe that transcending decision and involvement provides them with "freedom" by avoiding commitment. Nothing can be further from the truth. Deciding is a prerogative that is uniquely human. Only human beings are blessed with the ability to transcend instinctual dictates; we alone have choices.

Avoidance of issues; waiting for something to happen; looking back; depending on others to make decisions; compulsively going against the crowd or conforming to convention; procrastinating; impulse moves—all the forms of indecision and pseudodecision are destroyers of true inner freedom, self-realization and success.

As a psychoanalyst, I believe that everything we do has meaning and reflects who we are. The most important, making decisions, is illustrative of this truth.

A decision comes from the true self because all our decisions together define us.

If we make no decisions, we remain amorphous. We are nobody.

If we are blocked from emotional investment and decisive action, we are cut off from ourselves.

If we reject choice and commitment, we reject freedom.

You remember Captain Brown, whom I described earlier. Let me tell you one last thing about him. Several years after I left the navy, I inadvertently found out more about my commanding officer. He was considered a brilliant man, but never went beyond the rank of captain. Some years before I met him, he apparently failed to give an order and as a result beached a flotilla of destroyers. Late in his own career, he became a decision-maker. His principal decision was to help younger men like us to become decision-makers early in their lives, and thus to avoid disasters such as he had created.

II

The Decision Blockers

*W*hat makes someone abdicate the freedom to decide?

Decision blockers do. It is of utmost importance we recognize and understand these blockers before we go on to the stages of decision-making.

These major blockages to decision-making exist mostly on an unconscious level and inflict their insidious damage outside the victim's awareness. They overlap and permeate almost all aspects of our lives. But they are particularly destructive to the decision-making process.

These blockages, or "decision killers," as I think of them, almost never exist singly. Many and often all of them operate together and feed each other. As we neutralize any one of them, it becomes easier to tackle subsequent ones, because we loosen their interlocking symbiotic structure.

As with all emotional and physical difficulties, diagnosis is of prime importance. This is particularly true in the case of the psychological blocks I am about to discuss. Indeed, I believe that knowing, recognizing and understanding the decision blockers constitute the largest part of victory in the battle against them. It is almost impossible to fight against an unseen—and even worse, an unknown—enemy.

I will discuss the most powerful and most common decision blockages and go over particular problems they cause and suggestions for possible solutions. Solutions will also be touched on later, in Chapters 6 and 7. The blockages are not arranged in order of importance; they are all destructive. I am sure each of us can describe particular, individual blockages, but nearly all of them derive from the major one I will describe. I call these global because they affect all aspects of the personality's behavior and decision-making. This is especially true of the first five blocks.

The Decision Blockers

Global Blockage 1:   Losing Touch with Feelings

Global Blockage 2:   Resignation: Avoidance of Anxiety from Potential Conflict, or "Shunning the Whole Thing so as Not to Be Pulled Apart"

Global Blockage 3:   Having No Priorities, or Being Out of Touch with What Is and Isn't Important in One's Life

Global Blockage 4:   Lack of Confidence, or Poor Self-Esteem

Global Blockage 5:   Hopelessness/Depression/Severe Anxiety

Global Blockage 6:   Unrealistic Image of Self, or Self-Idealization

Global Blockage 7:   Self-Erasing, Inappropriate Dependency on Others, and the Obsessive Need to Be Liked

Global Blockage 8:   The Obsessive Quest for Applause and Mastery

Global Blockage 9:   The Dom Pérignon Syndrome: Perfectionism and Wanting It All

Global Blockage 10:   Sustaining the Chronic Belief That Something Better Will Come Along, Yearning for What Isn't While Demeaning What Is, and Wishful Thinking

Global Blockage 11:   "Nothing Ever Compares to What Exists Only in My Imagination" (But That Which Exists Only in the Imagination Doesn't Exist at All)

Global Blockage 12:   Fear of Generating Self-Hate in Anticipation of a Bad Choice

Global Blockage 1

Losing Touch with Feelings

*I*n psychoanalysis, losing touch with our own feelings is known as "alienation."

Alienation is a major defense against anxiety.

If we don't feel, we don't get hurt; we don't suffer from anxiety, anger or disappointment.

Unfortunately, this kind of defensive maneuver also removes us from our potential for joys of any kind, as well as for self-realization. And it is very damaging to decision-making.

Losing touch with feelings seldom occurs suddenly or through a conscious act of will. It is usually an unconscious process, which starts early in life and evolves slowly and insidiously as we get older.

Removing ourselves from feelings is just about always a response to a painful environment. This may include any number of situations, from overt hostility and rejection to subtle sabotage of our well-being and self-esteem early in life. Indifference, overpermissiveness, overprotectiveness, gross inconsistencies, injustices, favoritism, sadism and brutality are some of the underpinnings found in alienated people.

Many people who have lost touch with their feelings come from families in which feelings were hardly ever expressed. In some cases, the expression of feelings was either subtly or even opely condemned. This kind of environment, in which a virtual emotional vacuum exists, greatly undermines the evolution of feelings in a developing human being.

Alienation is pervasive and devastating to the decision process. I think of a friend of mine who is an excellent case in point. Christopher was a real estate developer, and a very successful one. As an adolescent, he had planned on becoming an artist. His father objected to this, so Christopher stifled his feelings about art. After graduating from college, he devoted himself entirely to business and to making money. By the time I met him, he had become "inundated by business affairs." Though he had become quite wealthy, his wife, Sara, and his children complained that he was "unfeeling" and "not there even when he was there."

It came as a shock, however, when Sara, saying that she was "tired of living in an emotional desert," announced that she wanted a divorce. Christopher had for four years been using his business affairs to escape from noticing how he or anybody else was feeling, and this was an unexpected blow. For several days, rage, grief and anxiety were overwhelming emotions. This was the first time in many years that he had felt strongly about anything outside the immediate business world.

In fact, Christopher's anguish was a healthy sign that he was not totally alienated from his emotions. If he had been able to let himself respond fully to the pain he felt, he and Sara might have talked about their problems and avoided a rupture. Unfortunately, he was unable to do this. Instead, he took an action designed to anesthetize him to his turmoil: He left his wife and children and got an apartment of his own. Of course, this solved nothing—it was a pseudodecision. Leaving his family and setting up on his own was not an action based on a genuine conviction that the marriage was hopeless. It was not based on any conviction at all. It was a maneuver that allowed Christopher to remove himself even further from his own feelings—this time literally.

Interestingly, however, the move turned out to be the beginning of a change of direction for him. When Christopher moved, he asked an interior decorator to choose some paintings for his new home. Generally speaking, there might be nothing wrong with this; seeking the help of an expert is often a good idea in gaining understanding of one's own priorities. But Christopher had once been an artist himself, and now he found himself unable to choose paintings for himself. He was, he realized, completely incapable of deciding what paintings to buy because he had deliberately dulled his feelings about art to the point of deadness in order to avoid conflict with his father's wishes. He felt nothing about art, not even dislike. He was unable even to *try* perceiving, feeling and deciding about something that had once been deeply important to him.

For the first time, he was frightened by his alienation. He had an inkling that there might be a connection between his removal from his feelings concerning art and what his wife had complained of in his behavior to his family. He became so upset that he decided to seek help from a psychotherapist.

I do not know whether Christopher ultimately worked out his problems with his wife. However, the decision to enter therapy was a probable sign of commitment to restoring the capacity for feeling that he had blunted over the years.

There are people much more alienated than Christopher who simply make no decisions at all. These individuals are truly lost to themselves and others. A prototype in literature is the main character in Albert Camus's superb book *The Stranger*, which describes a man who is a stranger to himself. He is more observer than participant in his own life. Even more severe cases include people who are totally removed from feeling to the point of being psychotic and catatonic.

But to the extent that any of us do not take our feelings and opinions seriously, we sabotage the decision-making process.

We can't make those choices unless we know that alienation exists and unless motivation is present. Sometimes a considerable jolt or an unexpected change in status quo will do it. A divorce, a death in the family, a birth, a financial loss, a windfall, sickness—anything that upsets an anesthetic balance may create anxiety and the possiblity of a reshifting. In a case like this, anxiety can be useful as a signal of difficulty and also as an innovating force.

People who have had extremely deadened feelings for a great length of time may need professional help. This usually is most effective in the form of psychoanalysis, in which a recapitulation of many of the causative trauma and difficulties can take place. This may be necessary to undermine the mind's deadening status quo and to start feeling again.

Of course, taking any feeling seriously and sustaining it helps. But the biggest help comes in the very process of making decisions. Making them, however great the initial struggle, is a necessary contribution to the revitalizing process.

I see alienation as an "umbrella block" under which many others cluster, because all of the other blocks, and indecision itself, contribute to putting us out of touch with feelings. Neutralizing the other blocks, therefore, puts us increasingly in touch with our feelings and undermines the self-destructive alienating process. Every real decision made has the same effect. When we really make the effort to discover our preferences and priorities, we initiate the process of knowing what we feel. We can begin to own ourselves.

Global Blockage 2

Resignation: Avoidance of Anxiety from Potential Conflict, or "Shunning the Whole Thing so as Not to Be Pulled Apart"

"Resignation" is the term used by Karen Horney to mean surrender to the current state of affairs in just about all areas of life. Resigned people cling tenaciously to things as they are.

As with alienation, which it resembles and feeds, resignation nearly always starts early in life with the attempt to avert great pain or internal conflict by avoiding involvement or emotional investment. Contractual agreements and commitments of any kind are seen as arch-enemies. Investment and commitment—including closeness to people as well as involvement with causes and activities—eventually produce enormous anxiety.

Individuals who are blocked in this way always see options and choices as having the potential for tearing them apart. Moreover, decision is felt as not only the essence of conflict but also a terrible, inundating entrapment. Choice and decision offer the possibility of change, thus threatening the safe harbor of a status quo.

We all employ detachment and resignation, as we do with every defense, to some extent. But there are those who make it a way of life. "Freedom" is important to them—but it is the wrong kind of freedom. This spurious freedom from emotional investment and involvement carried to an extreme becomes resignation.

Insight into this block is difficult, though not impossible. However hard potential decisions may be the dynamics of the resignation process always go on unconsciously. The process must remain unconscious because detached people are heavily invested in, and care very much about, sustaining an image of indifference to themselves. They take pride in transcending "trivial" human issues. Therefore, people who are trapped by this paralyzer often don't know it. Their lives always reflect their entrapment and they may complain bitterly about their impoverished existence. But they are seldom aware of their resigned status and the contribution they make to their own stultification.

Unfortunately, people blocked in this way often spend a lifetime with pseudodecisions that are nearly always made to promote noninvolvement and further stultification. They are continually backing into situations. Furthermore, detached people often have much difficulty in relationships, since mates, lovers and associates are frustrated by their seeming indifference and coldness.

Degree, of course, is very important here, as it is with any facet of human behavior. But the saddest part of this blockage, I believe, is that the avoidance of decision kills off most self-realization. Energy, time and self are so fully exploited in the service of avoiding the anxiety of commitment that none is left for the development of inner resources, proclivities and real self.

Awareness of this block is essential if decision power is to begin to develop. Motivation is important and sometimes occurs with an unforeseen imposition of an outside force or change, such as a death or a loss of a job. It also sometimes comes when misery is unbearable and is finally linked to an inability to choose, to decide to act.

Initially, attempts at involvement and confrontation with choice are fraught with anxiety. But people are seldom as fragile as they think they are. Anxiety is eventually replaced with satisfaction as decisions are actually made and the former victim of the block realizes that the dire consequences he or she imagined have not in fact occurred. As victims of this problem involve themselves at a deeper level in work and relationships, these become more enjoyable, involvement becomes less threatening, and decision itself easier and more fruitful.

Global Blockage 3

Having No Priorities, or Being Out of Touch with What Is and Isn't Important in One's Life

Not knowing our priorities is a major blockage, and a disaster as far as decision-making goes.

Most of us have no idea that we are in any way victims of this problem.

But not knowing where significant issues in life fall on a scale of personal priorities is an indication of an obscured value system. Understanding priorities tells in large part how we feel about ourselves and what we value as the important things in life. It tells about the use of time and energy, and about style of life. It tells what kind of people we can live and work with. Life's issues and the priorities they occupy constitute an area so important to decision-making that I will devote considerable time in the next chapter to discussing them. They are, in fact, the very foundation of decision-making.

Learning where issues lie on your own priority scale can take a lifetime of personal development and experience. Many of us, failing to realize that we have priorities, in effect don't have them at all. Avoidance of decisions, for any reason, feeds this blockage. Each time we abdicate from making a decision, we virtually declare ourselves without values and without priorities. This makes decision-making much tougher, completing a vicious cycle of enormous magnitude.

But each time we decide—really decide—we arrange issues in our lives according to a scale of priorities, and strengthen our self-knowledge.

Global Blockage 4

Lack of Confidence, or Poor Self-Esteem

*L*ack of confidence may seem obvious as a decision blocker, yet most people are unaware of it. It seems to them that an increase of self-esteem is a circuitous and distant route to effective decision-making.

But feeling even momentarily shaky about our judgment can interfere with decision-making. And chronic lack of self-confidence is absolutely devastating.

Sever ambivalence stemming from poor self-esteem is well known to psychotherapists. Indeed, a paralyzing inability to make decisions is often the only evidence psychotherapists need to know that they are dealing with more than usual ambivalence. While not all cases of *severe* ambivalence are directly due to poor self-esteem, there is at least an indirect connection.

Indecisiveness—especially in the form of jumping from one option to the other—comes from the underlying and usually unconscious feeling that no option which the person of low esteem chooses can be good, and that therefore another must be sought. Any choice made is no good by definition. He has not escaped; nor can he accept the choice he has made.

A low opinion of ourselves makes us feel poor because it robs us of success and happiness in all areas of our lives. Sadly, abdicating decisions and making choices born of poor self-esteem guarantees more poor self-esteem. On the other hand, risking decisions that are based on *realistic* self-appraisal almost always increases self-esteem.

Any kind of morale-boosting, any kind of realistic self-inventory, any halting of demoralization and self-deprecation, and avoidance where possible of relationships with people or activites that demean us will dilute this block and help the decision process. I feel that realistic self-evaluation is so important and helpful to self-esteem, in fact, that I've included a list of some Major Personal Assets for you to look at on pages 164–165.

Furthermore, risking decisions, especially those that express strong convictions about our own values and priorities, always increases self-esteem just as it builds awareness of feelings and the ability to become emotionally involved.

Global Blockage 5

Hopelessness/Depression/Severe Anxiety

*I*t is extremely difficult to function in any area of life when we feel hopeless. It is particularly difficult for a person in this frame of mind to make decisions.

Hopelessness as a blockage can never be considered in isolation. It is always accompanied by depression and anxiety. These three are bedfellows.

In evaluating the seriousness of the problem, degree must of course be considered. *Severe depression* is a clinical syndrome which always demands professional attention. "Decisions" that are made in this state may be highly destructive and designed to effect self-sabotage. They are really not decisions at all but compulsive moves against the self, based largely on intolerable anxiety and the hopeless belief that things cannot get better and that no change is possible. Self-hate and despair in this illness can take the form of suicide.

But more moderate and chronic feelings of hopelessness, depression and accompanying anxiety may be less obvious.

These feelings may have been present for so long that they are accepted as a way of life. Indeed, many of their victims do not know that they are depressed at all.

The source of the hopelessness and depression may be chronic disappointments following exorbitant expectations. By "exorbitant" I mean "not in accordance with what reality can provide." A business victory or graduation from college or publication of a book may bring money, open doors or provide artistic satisfaction. But if we expect these things to provide eternal health, endless life or guaranteed joy, we will be terribly disappointed.

Furthermore, false pride sets people up for repeated falls and hopelessness. People with poor self-esteem are always more vulnerable to self-hate. Eventually a good deal of anger accumulates—at one's self, at what often feels like an uncaring world, and at people to whom we relate. But in order to "get along" and "to make things work," we push most of this anger down—depress it—out of consciousness. Habitual "pushing down" is the main cause of chronic depression, in which all feelings are often submerged. Anxiety develops simultaneously because this suppressed and unrecognized anger threatens to surface into consciousness to destroy our nice-guy or nice-girl image of ourselves.

Regardless of the specific source, recognizing the condition is vitally important because it is always destructive to decision power, as it is to mental health in general. The inability to make decisions and the poor outcome of pseudodecisions contribute to hopelessness and its bedfellows, completing this very vicious cycle.

What are some of the signs of chronic and often hidden depression?

- Feeling "stuck": "Nowhere to go and no desire to go there even if there were a place"
- Chronic fatigue and inability to sleep

- Living life on "a muted level"
- Poor appetite and chronic underweight
- Chronic overweight and compulsive overeating
- Loss of ability to experience joy and pleasure
- The formation of destructive relationships
- A history of underachievement
- Loss of sexual desire and satisfaction
- Self-derisive and self-berating thoughts
- Much living in the past
- Chronic anticipation of disaster
- Chronic dissatisfaction with achievements; overachievement
- Chronic boredom
- Chronic guilt feelings
- Accident proneness
- Ever-decreasing productive functioning
- Inability to spend money on oneself
- Loss of sense of humor
- Preoccupation with illness and death

A particularly telling sign here is the increasing inability to make effective decisions despite valiant efforts. This is usually accompanied by an inability to bring various enterprises to successful completion.

Once the difficulty is recognized, anything and everything that can be done to lift morale is of value. Being kind to oneself is of prime importance. Doing things that used to be or eventually will be pleasurable regardless of how they feel now is helpful. So is doing *new* good things for oneself. Helping someone else who feels bad also helps us, because in doing this we muster our own resources. And *any* small decisions, leading even to the most minor successes, will help to begin to turn the tide.

It is *most important* to understand that chronic hopelessness and depression are not signs of a "weak character" or a "lack of moral fiber" or a "failure of nerve." They are symptoms of underlying difficulties, especially with anger and anxiety, for which self-knowledge and self-compassion are the best medicines. Short of getting professional help in this connection, you may find it useful to read another book of mine, *Compassion and Self-Hate*. Two other books that may prove helpful are *The Book of Hope* by Helen De Rosis and Victoria Pellegrino, and *Feeling Good* by David Burns.

Global Blockage 6

Unrealistic Image of Self, or Self-Idealization

To make things more complicated and difficult, many or even most people who suffer from poor self-esteem also suffer an unrealistically idealized image of self. This is a compensatory mechanism designed to cover up, and make up for, lack of feeling of self-worth. Unfortunately, it only serves to lower self-esteem and to further its hindrance of the decision process.

If our conception of ourselves is a valid one, we are fortunate indeed. As difficult as reality is at times, there is no substitute for its power as a constructive force. A rabbi recently told me that the great basic prayer of Jews is the request: "Please, God, help me to know myself." "Know thyself!" and "To thine own self be true" are superb pieces of advice.

But if my image of myself—unconscious, conscious, or both—is unrealistic, my decisions will suffer the consequences. As with the other blockages, degree is important. Few of us are completely deluded about ourselves. At the same time, none of us are totally realistic about ourselves. We all idealize ourselves, at least to some extent—perhaps as loving martyrs, or as masterful, benevolent helpers, or as freedom-minded independents. Most of us combine self-idealizing traits from many different possibilities. The effects of self-idealization can be positive: a loving martyr may become a Mother Teresa; a master and benevolent helper may grow up to be an Albert Schweitzer; a freedom-minded independent may make a mark as a great scientific or an artistic innovator.

Trouble is in store, however, when expectations of this "ideal" self become so inflated that, by comparison with the person's exaggerated standards, the actual self comes off poorly. If insecurity is bad enough, the drive to support the idealized self-image will become greater and greater. The "martyr" will unconsciously make decisions not on the basis of healthy feelings, values and priorities, but according to whether the outcome is likely to make him or her look like a martyr. The person with a deep need to support an inflated self-image of mastery will choose whatever course of action makes him or her *appear* successful, admired, a famous celebrity, or whatever the wished-for self-image happens to be. The "freedom lover" will unconsciously make decisions that support an exaggerated need to see herself or himself as a "free spirit" unconstrained by any emotional involvement whatever.

It is not at all unusual in unrealistic viewing of self for people to blow themselves up and sell themselves short at the same time. Such individuals commonly ignore and neglect their available assets even as they attempt to do things based on nonexistent skills and talents. Evaluation of self is off and choices will reflect this aberration, because judgment is distorted.

Those for whom failure is chronic despite a heroic output of energy and a belief in having made realistic decisions had better have a long look at themselves. This can be very,

very painful and it is not uncommon to need someone else, such as a trained psychotherapist, to help them do this effectively, through honesty and objectivity. Friends who have been persuaded into helping them perpetuate idealized self-images are worse than useless in this endeavor.

Reality may initially come as a jolt. A realistic view of self may at first feel like confrontation with a stranger. But the rewards of real and productive decisions have a soothing and healing effect and pave the way for self-acceptance.

Global Blockage 7

Self-Erasing, Inappropriate Dependency on Others, and the Obsessive Need to Be Liked

*T*hese blockages, which at a glance might appear to be distinct, actually are found in concert with each other. I will treat them individually, however, because in different people one may be more apparent than the other, and it's often easier to understand them separately.

Self-Erasing

Every time we abdicate decision-making in any way, and especially through dependency or the need to be a "nice girl" or a "nice guy," we erase ourselves.

Self-erasing means seeking emotional safety by not being there, and is part of the defensive strategy Karen Horney called "self-effacement." It is a form of living that makes no waves and discourages others from taking notice. On a practical level, it means drawing as little attention to oneself as possible. Usually this is the outgrowth of a desperate effort—possibly begun in earliest childhood—to avoid conflict or rejection by not drawing attention to oneself.

All of us have at least some familiarity with this defensive strategy. But when self-erasing becomes a principal strategy for coping with—or rather avoiding—life's conflict situations, tiptoeing through life becomes primary, as does drawing as little attention as possible to the presumably fragile, vulnerable self. On a deeper, emotional level, an investment in nonidentification of self develops: The self-eraser does everything possible to keep from appearing, to himself and to others, as an assertive human being.

This kind of emotional investment is a terrific decision blocker, of course. Indeed, if the blockage is severe, even the idea of a decision is enough to make the victim very anxious, including a paralyzing inability to make any decision at all. If a decision is for some reason unavoidable—for instance, if a life is at stake—and there is sufficient health to avoid or to break through a freeze-up, self-hate and considerable depression may ensue because of this enforced self-assertion. Perversely, the victim feels he has gone against himself.

You can readily see why people in this bind unconsciously choose indecision, or pseudodecisions that will combat the "threat" of self-assertion and perpetuate the status quo. Their '"decisions" are mainly of a variety that will prevent success and even guarantee failure. Self-erasers see failure as drawing less attention than success, thus producing less anxiety. They also see it as incurring less envy and therefore as less of a threat to being liked.

Finally, failure has plenty of potential for self-glorification through martyred suffering. The self-eraser can use his or her suffering as a manipulative tool to produce guilt. "See how much I've suffered for you; now you owe me love—and guidance." Freud's adage "In every fear there is a desire" is particularly applicable here. Even where there is a conscious wish for success and an accompanying fear of failure, there is also an underlying self-erasing desire to fail in "glorious" martyrdom. I want to emphasize, however, that although there is much self-humiliation to be found in the suffering of self-erasers, there is very little humility. Humility comes from self-awareness and knowing one's real limits and assets, not from self-humiliating martyrdom.

When victims of this problem do make "decisions," these are usually designed to satisfy a deep need to conform. Conforming aids the desire to get lost in the crowd to avoid notice.

But if the individual retains any health at all, he still wants success and happiness and can't understand why others get it and he can't. Of course, he is unaware of his inability to make the necessary constructive decisions because they threaten to throw him into conflict. Decisions—real ones—mean power, after all, and he has dedicated himself to the image of powerlessness and virtual non-existence.

Therefore it is extremely important that people suffering from this blockage take advantage of any opportunity at all to make decisions and to act.

Inappropriate Dependency on Others

This is a form of self-erasing and is, obviously, directly destructive to independent, personal decision-making; if we efface ourselves, we become more dependent on others.

This blockage is almost always found in concert with self-erasing and with the need to be liked. In most cases, reliance on other people's tastes, opinions and decisions is more apparent than self-erasing or the need to be liked even when all three are present. But in fact, it is extremely rare that we see these blocks singly and apart from each other. They spring from each other, and feed and support each other. Indeed, they can at times be indistinguishable.

Victims of obsessive dependency often reach a point where they almost never consult themselves. They simply "choose" the same option as the person or persons they depend on.

Such dependency is "inappropriate" because these people almost never lack the innate ability to make decisions. If their decision-making ability is crippled, it is because it has been in disuse for so long.

Clearly, a habit of this type is due to a lack of self-confidence and to poor self-esteem. But it may largely go on unconsciously. People with this blockage are often barely aware, and often not at all aware, of their infirmity.

People who habitually rely on others to make decisions for them often find ingenious ways of getting an "ally" to decide all sorts of issues that they are perfectly capable of deciding for themselves.

Of course, taking expert advice and consultation from others is not the same as blind obedience. The first are used in the service of decision. The second is used to avoid the process.

Difficult though it is to imagine, many people who suffer from such paralyzing freeze-ups are not aware that the origin of their paralysis lies in dependency. Yet dependency of this type is so common that whenever we are faced with paralysis in a decision situation, it behooves us to think at once of this type of dilemma and the grievous dependency it involves. The victim often has no consciousness at all of either dependency or "being pulled apart." On a conscious level, he or she may only be aware of being frozen and unable to reach a decision. This is often the time that a vicim of this habit-forming block will attempt to get still more opinions, count up more votes, seek out someone who is "stronger," "wiser" or otherwise impressive, so as to break the deadlock.

Obviously, this block cannot be removed unless the rationalizations stop and awareness of the difficulty replaces self-delusion. It is essential that victims of this block stop being afraid to rely on themselves, to take responsibility for their own decisions, and to live with the consequences, whatever these may be. In particular, it may be necessary to stay away from "strong" allies and "experts" for a while and to decide *no matter what*, in order to begin to break the dependency habit.

The Obsessive Need to Be Liked

The link between self-effacement, dependency and this blockage is "love." To merge with a self we perceive as fuller and safer than our own selves, we use "love" as the rationalizing binding glue. The more we are liked, the closer we can get.

This particular blockage can have an extremely destructive effect on all aspects of behavior. Practically everything one does is motivated by an insatiable need to be liked. Of course, the process of decision-making suffers inordinate damage as a result. Good decision-making is not consistent with winning popularity contests. In those of us who are very insecure, self-hating, dependent, and removed from our own feelings, being liked becomes the central issue of the decision rather than the substance of the choices themselves. If a good choice, a truly good choice, might produce dislike or if it is unpopular, it will either be abandoned for a bad one or a freeze-up with ensue.

To make matters worse, our culture reinforces the disproportionate worship of "love." Of course, mature love—by which I mean kindness, caring, openness, trust and intimacy—has great value. But even these constructive forces have serious limitations, and romantic love has very large limits as a basis for making serious decisions leading to either success or happiness.

All of us enjoy popularity, but the need to be liked reaches malignant proportions when it becomes an obsessive blockage. Being loved or being liked is seen as the solution to all problems and the only means of being safe. "If people love me they won't hurt me." In fact, victims caught in this bind are always hurting themselves through neglect of their own opinions and their own options. They also rationalize the damage they do to themselves by idealizing their goodness and "love" of others. Secretly, however, they also regard themselves as self-sacificing martyrs.

Sadly, nobody is universally liked all the time and no affectation, pretense, or twisting oneself into a pretzel produces a bit more love. Some people like us, some don't. In any case, most people can't stand phony manipulations for love; nor does the manipulator like himself.

When people with this problem find themselves in a situation where "love" is not forthcoming, they become confused, upset, and even less able to make independent decisions. Inhibition and paralysis are very common in this blockage because any decision is seen as a possibility for incurring disfavor. There is much repressed anger at people on whom they are dependent. There is much fear and anxiety of revealing that anger lest it threaten their being liked and their image as "nice" or "martyred." Thus their anger is expressed in subtle sabotage, mixed and confusing messages, disturbed relationships and misfired decisions.

Almost all of this goes on unconsciously, except the painful result of poor decisions and poor relationships. These are felt! However, when the individual can begin to question the value of the quest for universal love, he is on his way to the dissolution of this blockage. He must come to realize that being loved is a natural phenomenon which cannot be extended universally through any manipulation; that being liked is pleasant but has exceedingly limited value; that slavishness to this master wrecks the decision process. And he must come to realize that being liked has not in reality increased his safety or security one iota. He must admit and accept without self-contempt that he has been a prisoner of this blockage and that the energy and time used in this endeavor have been not only wasted but used counterproductively to rob him of decision power.

Global Blockage 8

The Obsessive Quest for
Applause and Mastery

*T*his is the other side of the coin of self-effacement. Paradoxically, it too is a reaction to and compensation for insecurity and deeply hidden poor self-esteem.

Liking applause is not in itself a blockage; every healthy person likes it.

But *addiction* to applause makes for terribly distorted decisions. The desperate need to be admired and to receive constant ego boosts (psychoanalysts refer to these as "narcissistic supplies") dictates decisions that are often antithetical to success and happiness.

Victims of this problem do make "decisions"—too many of them, too easily and too quickly. The steps in the decision-making process are often abbreviated to mere fragments or skipped altogether.

People stuck in this blockage want to be noticed; even negative attention means much to them. They would rather be noticed and disliked than liked and overlooked. Given the choice, they would rather be admired than liked. "How smart you are," "How beautiful," "How masterful," become their life's blood.

Mastery means a great deal to these people. But beneath their glory-seeking, their self-esteem is low and they have to protect it. They therefore are very prideful, and hurt pride brings great rage. They are often benevolent despots and can be very coercive and inundating. They are terrified of failure and humiliation and they avoid choices that risk injuries to pride. Being a winner at losing really frees us and gives us strength, but these are not modest or humble people; they are would-be big shots. Their decisions reflect all these characteristics. They often suffer from big highs and deep lows and incapacitating depressions.

Though relatively few of us suffer this blockage in the extreme, many sustain it to some extent. Whenever it is present, a compulsive need for applause tends to push all other goals aside in making choices. As one might expect with this kind of self-idealization or self-inflation, there is a great tendency to overestimate one's appetite, one's assets, one's capacity for struggle and perseverance and results. There is a tendency to extend oneself in every way and to expect extraordinary things from oneself and the world. Needless to say, this leads to poor decisions and a lot of disappointments.

Global Blockage 9

The Dom Pérignon Syndrome:
Perfectionism and Wanting It All

*T*hese two are so bad we ought to call them "super-blockages."

Perfectionists have a terrible time and they give everyone else a bad time too.

Beyond conscious awareness, they believe that there are perfect situations, that there are perfect decisions, and that the right combination of decisions will produce heaven on earth.

Let's face it: No decision is perfect. The only thing perfect about the human condition is its imperfection. But perfectionists evade this truth; they sustain the belief in the possibility and rewards of perfection.

Yet the very belief and quest for perfection keeps them impoverished! In fact, we might call this one the "Dom Pérignon Syndrome," because perfectionists are like people who would die of thirst in the desert before they'd drink water instead of the finest champagne!

Delays at every stage of the process are characteristic of

perfectionists. The delays are due to the attempt to have perfect conditions for making a decision and to "making sure" that the decision itself will be a perfect one. Fear of self-hate following imperfect results has at best an inhibiting effect and at worst a paralyzing effect. Perfectionists know nothing of their special kind of paralyzing grandiosity, their inhumane and inhuman approach to themselves and to the world; they think their standards are average and appropriate. Most of them do not think of themselves as perfectionists. But even as they proclaim humility, perfectionism swamps them.

This blockage would not be so important if it occurred only in full form, in complete perfectionists—that is, the relatively rare people whose obsession in life (like that of the character Felix in the TV series *The Odd Couple*) is perfection. But the fact is that this obsession affects all of us—some on a global level, others (fortunately) in fairly encapsulated areas. Wherever perfectionism occurs, it distorts judgment and is destructive to decisions.

It's important to understand that *excellence is not the same as perfection*. Excellence must above all conform with realistic standards. Otherwise it becomes a rationalization of obsessive, perfectionistic needs.

As with all the blockages, admission and acceptance of a serious problem are crucial here. Getting rid of this emotional difficulty requires realization that the more perfectionism permeates our existence, the greater is the struggle required.

When people first make the effort to appraise situations realistically, they often feel that they are giving up all standards and trading them in for an impoverished and shoddy existence. Of course, this isn't true. They are trading fantasy for reality and for acceptance of the human condition. The real swap here is action for paralysis, decisiveness for indecisiveness, and inner freedom for inner slavery. When this swap takes place and we prefer bread on earth to pie in the sky, the true quality of our lives improves a great deal.

Wanting It All: Sustaining the Illusion That It Is Possible to Realize All Options Without Paying a Price or Sacrificing Anything

Wanting It All is a special form of perfectionism, the search for heaven on earth. It is based on the unconscious belief that somehow a perfect state can be reached in which all options can be realized, so that painful choice and sacrifice can be avoided. It is also based on the unconscious hope that self-assertion through decision-making can be avoided. You can readily see how easily this fits in with self-erasure, and how susceptible to this blockage self-erasing people are.

These people really hope for a magic key that will unlock the door to their special nirvana. They are often stuck at an early stage in the decision process, that of having options or choices. The desire to realize all options blocks the process by making true choice impossible.

Wanting It All, in fact, often destroys the possibility of getting any of it, or getting that which would be realistically forthcoming from a decisive move.

The big, inhibiting, paralyzing illlusion here, which is largely unconscious, is that if you make no choice you will always have a chance to have it all. The Wanting It All victim is not unlike a small child in a toy store who can't make up his mind about a toy because he wants all of them. He finally has a temper tantrum and is dragged out of the store by his mother. Now he really screams, because he got nothing at all. This occurs with some frequency in people who desire mastery. Wanting It All represents the essence of mastery and the antithesis of helplessness, which they abhor. The drive to have it all leads to overextension of money, time, energy and talent, and to failure.

No change is possible here without insight and willingess to "pay." "Payment" in this connection is in the form of the discarded choices and dreams. The mental picture of a dream world of total possibility must be exchanged for one choice, one decision. Of course, one single working choice brings infinitely more real satisfaction than imaginary pie in the sky. Knowing this is crucial to motivation—and motivation is crucial to breaking through this and all blocks.

Global Blockage 10

Sustaining the Chronic Belief That Something Better Will Come Along, Yearning for What Isn't While Demeaning What Is, and Wishful Thinking

*T*hese are blood brothers to the last two blocks and really a perfectionistic extension of Wanting It All.

Endless delaying and waiting and still more waiting are characteristic here. As in other blockages, procrastinating often destroys the possibility of choosing good options, because time simply runs out. This usually leads to angry, grudging acceptance of "what's left," to grievous disappointment, and to still more exorbitant desires and waiting, completing another (characteristic) vicious cycle. Thinking something better will come along is sometimes used in self-erasure as a way of avoiding conflict, choice and success. It is also seen in detached, resigned people who use it to avoid commitment.

What is it that victims of this block hope will be better?

They are hoping for a mythical, comprehensive solution that will surpass all present choices combined. They wait for the option that will combine the virtues of all available options so that, in effect, nothing will be surrendered. If reasonably good choices are chronically passed up so that indecision causes all kinds of personal failures, we are usually dealing with this particular kind of poison.

The blood brother of hoping for something better is yearning for what's not there while demeaning what we've got. We all yearn for the past and at times we all long to have what just isn't possible.

Unfortunately, the process can get out of hand and become highly destructive. Feeling nostalgic is all right. But mentally destroying the here and now and being trapped in nostalgic reveries is definitely maladaptive and can produce profound inertia.

It can readily be seen that this block is related to all the perfectionism blocks, especially those I've just discussed. But here the dream is usually about specific goals that either can't be attained or are demeaned soon after they are attained. A woman, for example, may yearn to be eighteen again, or a sixty-year-old accountant may yearn to be a nuclear physicist; a man who longs all his life for a Cadillac grows to hate it soon after buying it because he suddenly feels it is "trash" compared to a Rolls-Royce.

This counterproductive process demeans whatever decision we make on just about any issue. It is a superb killjoy. When it is strong, its victim is so busy desperately wanting what he doesn't have that he cannot possibly appreciate or enjoy what he has.

Of course, decisions made without loyal, solid commitments are no decisions at all. They are generally shallow moves which only look as though they are born of real choice. If this reaction is severe and chronic, the victim may be so stymied by lack of real decision and resultant failure that he becomes paralyzed and achieves very little or nothing at all. This makes him yearn again for what he doesn't have, and so another vicious cycle comes into being.

Unconsciously these victims feel that anything they achieve or get isn't worth having because *they* achieve it.

This applies to the results of decisions too. Poor self-esteem and lack of awareness of what's really happening are at work here.

The other relative of fruitless yearning is wishful thinking, fantasizing that something that doesn't or can't exist might come to pass. Through "magical" thought, frustration and disappointment are made more tolerable as the impossible *seems* to come true.

Unfortunately, wishful thinking is often used as a substitute for decision. Like its fellows, Wanting It All and Yearning for What Isn't, wishful thinking does not produce anything but "false pregnancies." Instead, enormous energy and time go into this fruitless activity. Its victim does not understand why change does not take place. It does not because this is the stuff of suffering rather than the product of constructive struggle, creative imagination, or the thinking through of constructive ideas. Wishful thinking only contributes to living in the imagination. It is in effect nothing but destructive ruminating and has nothing to do with creative ideas which effective decisions can translate into real actions.

Global Blockage 11

"Nothing Ever Compares to What Exists Only in My Imagination" (But That Which Exists Only in the Imagination Doesn't Exist at All)

*T*his is also a blood brother of wishful thinking and the something-better syndrome. Its origin is often linked to pathological preoccupation with nostalgic forces of which the victim is not aware. There is a seeking for a time and mood that no longer exist and cannot be receated, relative to which current possibilities feel impoverished.

Living in the imagination comes, I suspect, from long-standing feelings of deprivation and the need to find heaven on earth as compensation. It is a block to reality and a destroyer of here-and-now living. It demeans the everyday joys of daily existence and makes success in any area of life an impossibility.

Global Blockage 12

Fear of Generating Self-Hate in Anticipation of a Bad Choice

*T*his one is extremely common, very malevolent, highly metastatic, and sneaky. It is malevolent because it often causes total abdication from the decision process. It is metastatic because it is fed by and feeds every other blockage and neurotic mechanism. Self-hate is used in the service of self-idealization. When we hate who we really are, we contibute to an idealized, unrealistic version of ourselves. Conversely, sustaining idealizations distances us from our real selves.

I describe this blockage as sneaky because, regardless of source, self-hate is mostly and often totally hidden. Its victim does not know, for example, that recrimination, second-guessing, self-glorification and illusions are forms of self-hate, and that he is idealizing himself. Therefore, the self-hate goes on doing insidious damage to the decision process as it remains hidden and safe from revelation and cure.

People with this blockage often suffer from what Karen

Horney called "arbitrary rightness," or the overriding need to always be right.

The overriding dynamic here is lack of confidence in, and loyalty to, oneself. People who suffer from it go into a vigorous self-hating mode and attack themselves at the slightest hint of an indiscretion or failure, however minor. They are often in terror of decisions and become totally impotent in making them because a "wrong" decision will bring on very painful self-hating attacks. Perfectionism, exorbitant expectations, need for total mastery and—at the same time—self-effacement, all abound here. These problems don't permit compassion or allow for human limitations and acceptance of choices that "go wrong." If the results are less than were demanded, such victims can and will inflict punishment on themselves. This can take the form of painful depression, psychosomatic illness, accident proneness, multiple failures, destructive relationships, insomnia, loss of appetite, overeating and a myriad of other self-punishments.

As I indicated earlier, most victims of this block are not conscious of its poison, though they may be aware of the resulting paralysis and symptoms. They really don't know why they are doing this or that; they are only fair-weather friends to themselves. Becoming conscious of the dynamics and substituting responsibility for guilt is extremely important. Substituting humility and reality for idealized glory-seeking and self-humiliation is curative.

Global Blockage 13

"Coulda, Woulda, Shoulda": Chronic Self-Hate from Being Swamped with Tyrannical Demands on the Self

*"C*ould have done that, if . . ." "Would have done that, but . . ." "Should have done that, only . . ." Second-guessing is the recriminating stuff of chronic, unrelenting self-hate—a cruel blockage par excellence. This block springs from all kinds of inner demands and contracts people unconsciously make with themselves. The demands, often conflicting, are forms of self-hate designed to make people feel more ideal to compensate for seeming deficits. Actually they dehumanize, confuse, demoralize, and obscure the clarity of necessary decisions. They produce a state of paralytic terror and fear of endless self-recriminations for breaking contracts with themselves of which conscious awareness may be utterly lacking. (For example: "I should be the smartest/the nicest/the most loved/the most masterful/the most understanding/the most entertaining.")

Choices predesigned for failure and born of self-hate and depression bring on still more recriminations and "couldas" and "shouldas."

People in this mess have to cast off the shackles of inner tyrannies or they will never be truly free. They must not indulge in the habit of berating themselves. As soon as they become aware of self-chastisement, recriminations and second-guessing, they must stop at once. To continue with this activity is the equivalent of feeding an emotional metastatis tumor. They must starve that tumor!

People plagued by this blockage must learn loyalty to and compassion for themselves no matter what they do or don't do, and regardless of the outcome of any decision or action in which they participate. They simply must turn off rage at themselves, no matter what the reason or what form it takes.

The chances are strong that their expectations of themselves and of life generally have been too great. This is true of many people, not only of out-and-out perfectionists. Greater familiarity with other people's assets and limitations may help victims of this block accept their own.

Professional help may be necessary too. Self-vilification and second-guessing can become an ingrained habit that is very difficult to root out. Making real decisions in a mood of self-recrimination is impossible, and the pseudodecisions that are made are always counterproductive. It must be remembered that optimism about self and the outcome of issues aids the decision-making process. This is so largely because it makes our inner resources and creative abilities more available to us.

Global Blockage 14

Option Blindness

Blindness to the availability of alternative choices and options cripples the decision process at its very inception. Without options, choice is impossible. What passes for choice is often a decidedly stunted version of it.

Option blindness is never accidental. Self-idealization and fear of conflict are the biggest feeders of this blockage and usually form its base.

The simple fact is that people turn off any creative machinery and vision in order not to see options that will be in conflict with idealized images of themselves. They also turn off options that will create conflict in any area and thereby produce anxiety. Thus victims of this blockage will not see an options that may incur someone's anger, if they need to see themselves as loved by everyone. They would rather ignore vital issues and be blind to realistic possibilities, even though this forces them into choiceless paralysis.

Option blindness often occurs under any kind of strong pressure. Pressure increases in crisis and in any stress situations: when we are tired or in poor health, or have too many masters to please. If options seem to be lacking, it is often wise, if possible, to postpone a decision until pressure is markedly reduced. Sometimes total rest and vacation are helpful, especially rest from the issue in question, before the decision is made.

Insight and courage are invaluable in overcoming this blockage. Acquiring them, however, usually involves considerable motivation and willingness to stop being a "loser."

It is important to know that we can't make everyone equally happy at the same time. We need to know that we must serve our own constructive needs first. This is not selfish! It does not exclude caring about others. Without a real self we cannot relate honestly and fruitfully to others or really help anyone else. Rabbi Hillel put it well two millennia ago. "If I am not for myself, who will be for me? But, if I am for myself alone, of what good am I? And if not now, when?" *Now*, in this case, must wait until a time when pressure is minimal. (Temporary postponement, of course, must not become a rationalization for endless procrastination.)

Global Blockage 15

Time Pressure Distortion and Panic:
The Illusion That There Is
Not Enough Time

*T*ime is a superb and practical safeguard against destructive, compulsive and impulsive moves.

Solid, practical choices are very difficult in moods of despair or ecstasy or extreme exhilaration. There are times when we have to "go with our gut" fast because there is no time. But "sleeping on it" also has its appropriate place. The necessity for instant, "command" decisions is very rare.

Usually there is more time than we think. There are issues in which evolution and clarification simply will not occur quickly. There is no substitute for time in these cases, and pressure for speed produces confusion and the need for still more time. This is especially true of relationships. It takes time to know people and to know ourselves in relation to other people. Decisions about marriage and business partnerships that aren't aided by ample time are likely to be based not on full information but on wishful thinking.

A self-imposed illusion that there is not much time is often used disastrously in attempts to break through inertia due to any of the other blockages. This can produce terrible pressure, leading to panic reactions. Panic is a supreme decision blocker since it prevents our tapping our resources and everything else we need to make a decision. I have found that a great deal of anxiety is generated by time pressure distortion. When the victim is relieved of the feeling of being "boxed in" by time, anxiety attacks often disappear very quickly.

So my advice is: Easy does it. There is usually plenty of time. Using time to feel things out, to mull things over, to relax when necessary as the evolution of a decision takes place, means using it well.

Global Blockage 16

Impaired Judgment

Poor judgment is directly destructive to good decisions and is very often a function of illusion. Good judgment—that is, the ability to evaluate choices rationally and in terms of the actual issues involved—is crucial to decision success.

Poor judgment is often the result of poor research and poor development of ideas. These are very common difficulties both in expansive, grandiose people and in impulsive people as well.

Nobody alive has good judgment all the time. However, emotional disturbance, especially of any severity, impairs judgment seriously. In states of despair, all alternatives will seem bleak and will distort judgment accordingly. In states of euphoria, seeing all options as wonderful is equally destructive. The same is true of severe stress and powerful conflictual states of mind.

All of the blockages discussed, however, have a deleterious effect on judgment, and the damage is usually directly proportional to the intensity of the blockage.

The most basic ingredient of good judgment is an objective view of reality itself, and of ourselves. Without that, our view of everyone else and the world and everything in it becomes distorted.

Global Blockage 17

Lack of Inner Integration, or "The Chairman Is Missing": Severe Disorganization

*T*here are times in everyone's life when we may go through short periods of more than usual emotional upheaval. For all of us, these are poor times to make decisions.

The blockage of severe disorganization, however, is a fragmenting weapon. People may suffer it in common even though the origin and severity of their illness may be different. There are severley disturbed people who are able to function and those who can't function at all. There are those who are totally removed from their feelings and are quite delusional and irrational, and others whose logic remains intact but who are beset by strange feelings and delusional beliefs. There are those who sustain quick cycles of enormous mood swings, and others whose moods remain fairly stabilized but are inappropriately flat or euphorically high.

It's as if the chairman is missing. The chairman is the one who, in healthier people, can listen to each autonomous desire, each need, each argument; the chairman applies experiential knowledge and judgment and comes to a reasonable conclusion. But chronic intrusive thoughts, conflicting interests, absence of a strong sense of self, and no feeling for priorities make integration of all aspects impossible. This negates the possibility of real decision.

In most of these cases, treatment is necessary so that the therapist can exert influence in supporting the development of a mature, integrating force. This can only be done as quieting down takes place so that the individual can hear and feel himself and get to know who he really is and what he really wants. Eventually, prioritizing must take place and this aids the birth or rebirth of a benevolent chairman.

The Big Fact

*R*ecognizing, accepting and then neutralizing blockages is the first major step toward successful decision-making. The next step is establishing solid, fully conscious knowledge of our priorities. This facilitates, and is crucial to, every decision we make. In the next chapter, I want to discuss how we can enlist this knowlege of self in the service of decision. But before that let me give you some very important advice, which I call the Big Fact, and which I believe is essential in evaluating your own role in the decision-making process as you go through it in this book.

The Big Fact about decision-making is absolutely central to the entire process of becoming a real decision-maker.

The Big Fact is this:

In very few instances is one decision actually better than another.

In the majority of issues, almost any choice can be converted into a constructive decision. You've probably heard people say this often. But what does it mean? It means a number of very important things.

1. Above all, it means that in most issues, very few options would make "bad" decisions. There are exceptions, of course, but few choices are discarded because they represent "bad" choices. Some choices become discarded choices not because they are "bad" but because no matter who we are, we simply cannot have it all. An option becomes a discard through the process of our withdrawing our investment—ourselves—from it.

2. By the same token, an option becomes a decision through the process of our dedicating ourselves to it and iinvesting ourselves in it. Our loyalty and commitment to the decision is what this core of decision-making is all about. Aside from grossly inappropriate decisions, pseudo-decisions and coercive decisions, it is not the choice itself that makes or breaks the decision. The decision-maker makes or breaks the decision according to the strength or weakness of commitment and loyalty to the choice.

3. You make it work! It almost always is the decision-maker and not the particular choice that makes the decision work. If it doesn't work, the problem almost always lies with the decision-maker, and the decision will not succeed regardless of which choice is made. I repeat the salient point: *The failure of the decision has little or nothing to do with the choice. The failure is directly traceable and proportional to lack of dedicated commitment.* Most choices or options have their good and bad points. Choices are good only if we make them good. Some require increased adaptation effort, but our loyalty to them will make this effort possible. This devotion of our time, energy, hope and struggle to the cause at hand is crucial.

4. Loyalty to a decision is directly proportional to loyalty to ourselves. Thus we should not turn on ourselves when the going gets rough or difficulties present themselves.

5. The first essential of the successful decision is to make a decision. The entire process springs from the underlying, permeating belief that making decisions is all-important in being a full person. Therefore, the all-important decision is to make decisions, real and free ones. Making decisions is almost always more important than the substance of the decision itself, which is why most choices will be equally satisfactory as long as dedication exists. Conversely, making no choice, or indecision, invalidates all options because it paralyzes the victim. But the more we make decisions, the more natural the process becomes.

That decision-making itself is the most important aspect of decision-making is part and parcel of my belief that living is the most important part of living. Each decision affirms the statement "I exist here and now!" Every time we commit ourselves to our own choice, we affirm the biggest decision of all, the *decision to live*.

III

Priorities: Applying Who We Really Are to the Decisions We Make

The Common Priorities

I have discussed priorities in almost all the other books I've written because they are so important in understanding human problems and solutions. In *One to One*, I spoke of the importance of examining the commonality of crucial priorities in couples in establishing the prognosis of relationships. The question of priorities has no greater significance than in the area of decision-making of any kind.

Priorities—the position of life's issues on our personal scale of importance—tell us more about our real values than anything else. In effect, they explain us to ourselves in terms of real, everyday, practical issues. To ignore priorities makes for disastrous decisions. As I explained earlier, being out of touch with priorities is one of the major blocks to decision-making.

Some people have priorities. Even if they don't consciously know what they are, nevertheless they use them as a basis for decisions. Other people, however, are out of touch with their feelings and therefore out of touch with any sense of priorities. Their chaotic choices reflect this.

The relative importance or unimportance of priorities is not a trivial matter. To a great extent, we *are* our priorities, and this is why priorities are not changed easily. Priorities can change, and it is good to be flexible enough to change them when healthy growth requires this—but for the most part they enjoy a marked stability. We feel very strongly about our tastes and values even when we are not fully conscious of them.

In this chapter I will attempt to give you insight into your priorities and to help you determine where different issues stand on your own scale. I will discuss priorities that are common and form the basis for a great many decisions. It is important to realize that *different people have different priorities*. I will list and discuss many here, but the order in which I discuss them is not significant. All that counts is their value to you.

Health, Sex, Family, Work, Money, Sociability Versus Solitude, and Children come first because I consider these issues universal. That is, nearly everyone has to grapple with them sooner or later in life. The remainder are among the most common priorities. You may want to add others that have personal importance for you.

Think of them as being on a scale from 1 to 10. The highest priority is 1, and 10 is lowest. Rating them according to where they stand is an invaluable exercise in recognizing who we are and what we want out of life.

Being honest is vital. This means asking how we really feel about these issues, not inventing some glorified or falsely humble version of how we think we *ought* to feel about them.

The Common Priorities

Health

Sex

Family Life

Work

Money

Sociability Versus Solitude

Children

Security

Prestige, Power and Recognition

Education

Ownership (of Property or Material Things)

Roots, Tradition and Ethnicity

Religion

Physical Activity

Intellectual Activity

Creative Activity

Appearance

Excitement, Stimulation and Variety

Pleasure

Romance

Relaxation

Feeling Good and Freedom from Stress

Physical Comfort and Convenience

Integrity

Quality of Time

Weather

Health

Most of us want to be healthy. For some of us, sustaining health is a way of life and nothing takes precedence over it.

A fifty-three-year-old woman I know—whom I'll call Mary Smith—underwent cancer surgery several years ago. Chemotherapy was recommended as part of the postoperative treatment. Mary was told that her life would be prolonged by the chemotherapy, and eventually her health (which was poor following surgery) might also improve substantially. But the treatment itself would bring major, prolonged discomfort—even a good deal of suffering.

Mary considered the options carefully. She consulted several specialists. Each opinion was consistent with the first. She realized that health and life extension were of very high priority to her—higher than physical comfort. Freedom from pain and stress were high too, but lower down on her list. She chose chemotherapy. Her life has been prolonged; interestingly, she has also increased her peace of mind. "I would have had a hard time," she told me, "living with the knowledge that I hadn't done everything possible for my health."

However, as a physician, I do find that many people who

say that health is a prime consideration go on to demonstrate quite the reverse with smoking, overdrinking, drugs, reckless driving, overeating, no exercise, overstressed lives, terrible relationships.

If you believe health is a high-priority item, make decisions accordingly and act on them.

Sex

For some people, sex is the very essence of their being. For others, sexuality occupies a place on the lowest rung of the ladder. Unlike the sexually highly motivated person, they may experience intimacy, openness, tenderness, trust, caring and all other feelings—envy, possessiveness, warmth, anger, infatuation—in a relatively nonsexual way.

For most of us, sex probably falls around midscale, and in different circumstances and times of life goes up or down a notch or so.

But here again many people are confused about their feelings. A great many simply do not know consciously what they feel. Others refuse to admit and to accept the real truth about the importance or unimportance of sex in their lives.

I have interviewed any number of people—of both genders—who perceive themselves as valuing sex highly but who really are quite neutral about it. I have seen many people who are quite prudish and who spend a lifetime believing that sex is of minor interest when in truth they have sexual fantasies constantly and sexualize everything.

I have seen any number of people who believe that all other people are as sexual or nonsexual as they are. They see everyone through their own glasses and can't possibly believe that great variety and priorities exist.

The truth is that marriage and long-term relationships are

not for everybody. And some people can only live with others sexually in exclusive relationships. Mutual attraction is important. But where sex stands on the priority lists of two different people who are contemplating a sexual liaison is more important, as far as their prospects for a successful relationship are concerned, than the fact of mutual attraction. Knowing that is crucial to effective decision-making in this area.

Family Life

I believe that the feelings which ensue from being a part of a family occupy a position of very high priority for the majority of people. I include the many problems along with the joys that can be found in family relationships.

That family life occupies a high priority rating is understandable, since most of us spend our infancy and most impressionable years with our families. This may well account for why we take our feelings about family for granted and are not always fully conscious of the high priority it may have for us.

Obviously, decisions based on appropriate prioritizing in this area are of extreme importance. They involve marriage, responsibility, commitment, intimacy, relationships, the hierarchy of importance of various people (relatives and nonrelatives), kinds of economic lives chosen relative to social needs, money needs—and almost everything we can think of that goes into style of life and day-to-day living.

Ignoring how we feel about this priority can lead to very complex, difficult and nonadaptive life choices. Trying to convince ourselves of what is not true because we think it is expected of us is counterproductive. This priority can and does change, but most often does not. Unless it does, decisions are better made that respect the current truth.

An interesting illustration is Bill and Georgia, a childless pair in their late thirties. Bill teaches political science at a local college and Georgia has a responsible position with a performing arts organization in the city. A few months ago, Bill was offered a full research professorship at a university in a state farther west. It was an interesting position and carried with it good pay, prestige and some administrative power in the university. Best of all, Georgia would not need to uproot her own career; Bill could work out an arrangement with the university that would allow him to commute during the semester and be in New York every other week. One or two friends urged Bill to accept the position. He and Georgia had no children, they pointed out, and the job was a plum that could lead to better things. But Bill and Georgia decided that he would turn down the offer. Precisely because they had no children, they felt, it was important to them both to spend time together and also with their families, to whom they were close geographically and emotionally.

If family life had had a lower priority rating for either or both of them, other priorities might have won the day—the pay, security or job satisfaction Bill would have had. But family life happened to be their top priority, winning out over all the others for both of them.

Work

Our feelings about work can be complex. The kind of work we do has much symbolic significance; it also plays a role in our status at the office, in our neighbourhood, with our circle of friends, and in our own minds.

Where work stands for us on a scale of priorities is also crucial to many decisions affecting time spent with family and leisure time; a sense of fulfillment and responsibility; achieving the desired standard of living; where to live.

For some people, whose identity is closely involved with what they do for a living, work is the center of life. The right work for them is meaningful, uplifting, and therapeutic.

Conversely, some people do not have a profound emotional investment in *how* they earn their living. They may have no interest in working all the time. For others, if they have to work for any reason—to earn money—their lives become hell and they are miserable. Their investment and self-identification are elsewhere.

Money

There is no one in our society who sees money simply as money and nothing else. Some see it as representative of time and work. Some, for good or ill, see it as symbolizing love, or as a means of getting the world's attention. Some see and use it as a way of exerting control over family, friends and associates. Money has a vast range of symbolic associations; among the more common ones are power, status, security, expertise, longevity, immortality, freedom, maturity, energy and self-esteem. For the most part, few people are free of the symbolic influence beyond money's immediate, practical value.

One's valuation of money affects almost all daily decisions involving small and large matters—shopping, investing, saving, borrowing, lending or venturing. And how we handle money matters and decisions is largely influenced by the kind of people we are: secure, scared, impoverished-feeling, generous, adventuresome, etc.

The problem is that many would-be decision-makers are either unaware of or deny the great role of money in their lives. This makes for choices and pseudodecisions replete with duplicity, misunderstanding, thwarted expectations, mutual inappropriate claims, disappointments, angers, manipulations, self-hate, and feelings of insignificance and impotence. Attempts to transcend the importance of money or to obfuscate its importance—"I don't really care about the money part of it"—lead to misunderstandings and failed decisions.

Whatever our unconscious attitudes about money are, it is vital to good decision-making that we recognize them and that we be aware of money's real status for us.

Sociability Versus Solitude

There are socializers and there are "hermits." Socializers enjoy belonging to organizations, hobby clubs, health clubs, professional associations. They hang out around the office coffee machine during breaks and they frequent the faculty lounge and they like PTA meetings. They revel in party-going. They hate being alone.

Hermits are just the opposite. They may like warmth, intimacy and openness with others, especially those close to them, but they need solitude. They can be isolationists. They like working alone—at home, in a library, out in the garden.

Actually, almost no one is exclusively one or the other. Most of us are gregarious at some moments and hermits at others. But usually one or the other attribute predominates. And since we live in a world of people, decisions that affect the degree of social contact or solitude in our work and personal lives come to all of us sooner or later. Knowing our priorities in this regard is absolutely crucial.

I recall a patient of mine who, after many years of working as a financial analyst in a bank, decided to quit and start up an investment business with a partner who had been at the same bank. Both men were good at their work. But the partner, who had been accustomed to dealing with customers and thought of himself as extremely social, found that he "couldn't stand having to drum up business all the time." He realized that what he had wanted all along in leaving corporate life was to get away from the constant social pressure of three-martini lunches. On the other hand, my patient—who had always congratulated himself on being "independent," a "loner"—discovered that he hated working at home, cut off from contact with people in an office. After a considerable financial loss on both sides, as well as resentment, the partnership was dissolved and my patient returned to his job at the bank.

There isn't a single area of life that is not influenced by our feelings about our closeness to, or distance from, people. Knowing and honestly admitting and accepting our values in this respect can both avert disaster and give us an enormous advantage in making real, and successful, decisions.

Children

For some people, children are everything, and family life means nothing without them. Others, regretfully or gladly, feel that they are better off without them.

Convention exerts a superpowerful force here! Many people who have children feel coerced into having them, and then proceed to destroy the children and themselves. They want a family, but they don't want children. Unfortunately, they do not resolve this dilemma by thinking it through and coming to a decision based on a hierarchy of priorities.

I know a couple who have had two children in their six

years of marriage. They "don't really know how it happened—it just did." The wife had children because it was "the thing to do." The husband wanted children "because the wife did." In reality, they were both complying with the wishes of family members on both sides who wanted them to have children. They realize now that they didn't really want children. They are envious of their childless friends. They are dutiful parents, but there is little warmth or intimacy between them and their children. I have no doubt that because of this, their children will grow up with little capacity for joy, with poor self-esteem and much feeling of emptiness.

The simple fact is that children are a lifelong responsibility for which not everyone is prepared. For many people other priorities take precedence, but they don't know this. We ought to have children only if having them is top priority! We can only know for certain if people are top priority if we ask ourselves the question *before* the intent becomes a fact.

Security

The human condition precludes the possibility of total security. The title of James Watts's wonderful book *The Wisdom of Insecurity* tells it all.

Of course, some degree of security—financial, emotional (in relationships), physical—plays a role in all our lives, and priorities in this regard will vary. It is not accidental that there are more office job holders than independent entrepreneurs and that so many people seek the security, illusory or otherwise, of tenured positions in civil service employment. Some people are also tradition-minded and prefer tried and tested activities to new experiences, especially those involving risk.

People who are insecure and who have poor self-esteem, largely as a result of difficult early lives, tend to place security on a much higher level than others. When its standing is high, it cannot be ignored and must take precedence over other considerations. If it is ignored or not properly heeded, some painful anxiety will be generated.

Prestige, Power and Recognition

These three are Siamese triplets, and high priority in one usually means high priority in the others, though one or the other may be slightly higher on the scale.

Since I also discuss freedom from stress and peace of mind as priorities in this book, let me say that if we lower the priority value of "PPR," we almost always lower our level of stress. If PPR is high on the scale and we fool ourselves into believing otherwise and make decisions based on a low PPR position, we will inevitably provide much more stress for ourselves. Here, as elsewhere, choices that are inconsistent with real priority standing make for civil war within us and for self-hate and unhappiness.

I have known people who perceived money as the all-important factor of PPR that would make up for everything else. But despite its high symbolic value for them, it just didn't. Others fooled themselves into believing they were simple, lucky, benevolent people who couldn't possibly be interested in PPR. Of course, this was untrue.

Conversely, I have also seen a number of people for whom PPR was top priority and who had a good deal of it, but what they had was never enough to compensate for their feelings of inadequacy. When some of these people fell from positions of "grace" through their own poor choices or through events that occurred outside their power, the crash to earth was devastating. (This crash is especially terrible in high narcissistic people to whom stardom or fame in their field of activity is of prime importance.)

In any case, if this is a top priority, it's better to know the fact than to deny it.

Education

Where education is top priority, it is interesting to note how much people will do to promote this priority for themselves and for those close to them. There are times when this means great expenditures of money, energy and time.

If choices are made that neglect educational pursuit when this is a top priority, the price paid in terms of self-realization can be enormous. Neglect of education often leaves a terrible longing for what could have been, and chronically poor self-esteem.

Incidentally, I am often struck by a notion many people have that if they don't take the time to go to school, time will somehow stand still. "But that will take four years," they say. The four years will pass whether they go or not, and if they *decide* to go they will have a degree and will feel better for it.

Ownership (of Property or Material Things)

For many of us, ownership has high priority. We need to own a video recorder or a speedboat more than we actually need the objects for use. How many of us have clothes never worn, tools never used, possessions never enjoyed?

I have a friend who says he couldn't care less about owning anything—"only people count to me." But his huge home is a burglar's dream come true. He has collections of collections, and never has enough. He never parts with anything.

So honesty about where we stand here is important to our decisions. Ignoring a deeply felt need for certain possessions may just make us feel miserable and impoverished. We must let ourselves in on how we really feel about material possessions; this helps good decision-making immensely.

Roots, Tradition and Ethnicity

There are many, many people in the United States for whom these factors hardly exist on their priority scale. But there are other people for whom roots, traditions and ethnic heritage (geographical considerations, family customs, family business, food, etc.) have absolute primacy.

I knew one young man who could not get into medical school and was devastated. What came out when we talked was not his love of medicine but his need to become a doctor because he came from a long line of doctors. This priority topped all others. However, he was young, healthy and flexible enough so that he could move this priority down the list.

The fact that a priority occupies a high or a low place, because of either healthy internal pressures or brainwashing from without, does not alter its status or its effect. It usually takes hard work and considerable struggle to change its position on the scale. But ignoring its real position brings bad consequences.

Religion

Interestingly, many people do not know how strongly they feel about religion. Some are almost totally out of touch with their strong feelings, but this does not neutralize them. For others, belonging to a particular religious group is the mainstay of their identity. Knowing it, obviously, has great relevance in decision-making involving marriage, children, social involvements, where to live and economic decisions.

I know one family whose life is largely influenced by their church, and religious activity has very high priority. They chose a house near their church and occupations that do not interfere with church tenets. They married within their church. They have friends outside their church (including me), but much of their social life is with church members. Their decisions bring happiness and they feel peaceful and close to God.

Conversely, I know another family who belong to the same denomination, but for whom religious practices and church activities have a priority of about 8; they attend church meetings rarely. Their friends, marriages and economic decisions have little or nothing to do with religion. They are happy with these decisions because, like the first family, they know where they stand in this regard.

There are a number of people who try to transcend religious identification and influence. If they have strong feelings about religion and try to ignore them, their choices will generate difficulty. If feelings about religious identification have indeed changed, then their decisions will be healthy ones. However, illusions change nothing; they only make for bad choices.

Physical Activity

Physical activity and intellectual activity are constantly polarized in our society.

Families, and teachers too, pressure and lock children into compartmentalized roles which they are sometimes stuck with for their entire lives.

Let me emphasize, because it is so important, that you can be good at both and most of us need both.

If physical activity is a high priority, decisions that ignore and preclude the possibility of its fulfillment turn into disasters. There is little as tormenting to a person who needs, really needs, to move as being locked to a desk. The same applies to a physically active person who has a partner who does not like physical activity and gets to seem like dead weight to the more active person. The less active partner often suffers too, feeling constantly coerced and pushed into doing things he or she simply doesn't like.

Children who do not care for sports or who have been taught to equate sports with masculine strength are especially apt to suffer from being coerced into physical activity. Martin Symonds, a colleague of mine who is a child psychoanalyst, tells me that he is convinced that many physical injuries in children occur because the children really don't want to participate in sports. Is it possible that the same occurs in adults who are coerced by convention and an idealized image that they must live up to, when this one really has a low place on the priority scale?

Intellectual Activity

There is a vast difference between having a good or even a super intellect and being an intellectual.

There are any number of people who have excellent intellectual endowment but very little intellectual interest.

There are people for whom intellectual interest and involvement take absolute top-drawer priority.

People who like to use their minds and who love the world of ideas, books, music and museums may like physical activity as well. But if at work, at play or at social gatherings they are with people who are not intellectually stimulating, they will be miserable.

This is a very useful priority to determine about ourselves, but it is not an easy one. When I question patients about how and with whom they like to spend their time, their answers often do not jibe with their conceptions of themslves. Many self-hating intellectuals see themselves as non-intellectuals because they are not creative geniuses or intellectual giants. Their standards can be fantastic. Many non-intellectuals idealize intellectuals and see themselves as less than smart or even 'stupid' because they lack interest in intellectual areas. Some people obviously idealize intellectual activity, while others feel that all "eggheads" are ridiculous, impractical visionaries. Many such ideas are fed by a media-influenced culture. These beliefs and prejudices and self-prejudices make for distortions and confusions. It therefore behooves us to be very careful in our self-evaluation. Going against natural proclivities can result in a style of life that is cruelly stultifying and burdensome.

Creative Activity

The need for self-expression through art, music, acting, writing, etc., can exert an overwhelming influence. When it is powerful, it often demands exclusive attention, or at least center stage, in just about all areas of life.

Creative people who are strongly influenced by outside forces to lead conventional lives devoid of creative work make disastrous choices. This is truly the stuff of chronic depression. Where the desire for creative activity exists at all, healthy survival demands at least some energy and time investment in creative enterprise. Decisions based on this reality are life- and health-affirming because neglected inner resources don't simply go away; they form emotional abscesses that poison the entire person.

Again, parents must be careful in the decisions they make relative to this priority. A parent for whom creative work has high priority must not bring inappropriate pressure on a child, or foster inappropriate expectations. This may start an endless process of self-hate in a child who is not creative and cannot provide the needy parent with vicarious satisfaction.

A parent for whom this item has low or no priority must be careful not to neglect, let alone discourage, a child who is truly artistic. This leads to seriously disturbed relationships between parent and child and often to emotional disturbance of serious consequences when the child grows to adulthood.

Appearance

Knowing you place a lot of value on someone else's appearance can save a lot of trouble, since what you see is not always what you get.

People for whom looks (their own and/or others') are top priority and who don't know it or deny it can of course make some disastrous decisions based on very shallow and superficial considerations in social life or the choice of a mate.

On the other hand, for some people, appearance, for good or bad, occupies such a high position on the priority scale that decisions made against this priority may have adverse consequences.

And, too, high priority in this area—say, when it is a 1 or a 2—can sometimes result in a preoccupation that blocks development and evolution of other assets. Such narcissism is readily transmitted to young children. Children of highly narcissistic people may suffer the consequences of considerable stunting and can be relegated to very shallow living.

While looks may be important, unless we are professional 'lookers'—models or actors—that importance is limited. Development of other proclivities and skills is necessary for most of us, both socioeconomically and for general interest in life.

Excitement, Stimulation and Variety

The position of these on the priority scale dictates life-style, including how we choose work and lovers, to an enormous degree.

But even the most rabid stimulation addicts are seldom

aware of their need for excitement and variety. This uncon-
sciousness may go on despite a lifelong history of self-
manufactured crisis situations especially designed to create
stimulation of one kind or another. These are people who
are often on the brink and sometimes fall off.

Living with a person whose need for stimulation is high
can be murder for someone who values security and peace
above all. If a potential partner is at all suspect in this area,
it is wise to investigate fully before commitment is made.
By the same token, the "high-priority person" here sees the
"low-priority person" as a "drag," or "bore," and a "party
pooper." If they are not too disparate on the scale, one
partner can provide interesting stimulation while the other
provides necessary equilibrium. But if the priorities here
are widely disparate, life will be torture for both.

Of course, the same is just as valid for would-be business
partners, and it is of great importance to understand this
before commitment to partnership or business deals takes
place. The fact is that some people are more motivated by
excitement than by profit. Interestingly, some people understand this about potential partners without direct questions.
They know the person's business history and develop a
perception of him during interviews. But in order to truly
know the other person, in any area, it helps to know
ourselves.

Pleasure

Believe it or not, we are not all pleasure oriented. There are
those of us who are more interested in being fairly comfortable and anxiety free than in seeking pleasure.

But there are people to whom sensual enjoyment means
almost everything, for whom the pleasures of dining and

traveling, viewing art and theater, listening to music, and so on are the most important pursuits in life.

Of course, many of us enjoy things of the senses. But remember, it's a question of degree.

Having similar priorities in this area is an important basis for happy relating, and it behooves potential partners to understand how they feel about this issue; it will in large part determine how their days and nights are used.

Romance

Many people who see themselves as romantics are actually not, and many who *are* romantics don't really know it. Many people like a safe, secure, prosaic and routine home existence. Others live for trips to exotic places, meeting various kinds of people, sky diving, reading poetry together, or other romantic activities.

People who place romance high on their priority scale sometimes have a capacity to see adventure in the commonplace and to appreciate the uncommon when it is presented. They have imagination, but there are those who live in the imagination to the detriment of reality.

Decisions involving types of work and love liaisons are much affected by this priority. Even the most imaginative romantic will be unable to move unromantic people, or to transcend jobs in which romance is of very low priority. Attempted commitment to situations and people dedicated to the prosaic and concrete eventually causes dissatisfaction, distress, and depression.

People who can enjoy the enthusiasm and charm of the romantic as well as stability are well balanced.

Relaxation

Relaxation comes in many forms. The enormous differences this one occupies on our scale of priorities is interesting.

For many people, relaxation has very low priority. They can talk about it and understand it intellectually but on a true gut level it doesn't exist; if they are forced into "relaxing," the resulting strain and irritability can be enormous. For others, relaxing has absolutely highest priority.

Taking the value of relaxation into account in work and personal life, especially in a choice of partners, is crucial, because the extremists in these two groups often have difficulty empathizing with each other. *Going with ourselves* makes for real success and happiness and a long, healthy life, which is impossible when we knowingly or unwittingly *go against ourselves*.

Feeling Good and Freedom from Stress

Being absolutely free from anxiety and stress is an impossible achievement. One would think that all of us want to feel good as much as possible. But if we give precedence to decisions that put us at risk (e.g., take chances with anxiety-producing business deals): (1) we may not know enough about ourselves and our vulnerability to anxiety; (2) we may not know that being relatively anxiety free has great value for us; or (3) we may think freedom from stress has value but not know that other items (e.g., power, prestige, recognition and stimulation) have greater value.

I am reminded of a man I saw a year ago who felt chronically anxious and "under the gun" and who certainly did not "feel good." He claimed he had come to consult me for that reason. This man went on to say that he had been married three times and had seven children. He had great difficulty supporting all his dependents. Yet he was contemplating marriage to a woman twenty years his junior, whose top priority was having several children! I advised him to take a look at his list of priorities and ask himself whether being anxiety free meant enough to him to prevent his entering into this new commitment.

If feeling good and being relatively anxiety free are really of top priority, then we must take all of our priorities seriously. We must take ourselves and our well-being seriously. I do not suggest caution to the point of paralysis. But particularly where we have a history of choices leading to more than usual anxiety production, I suggest looking for self-hate and self-destructive tendencies. In any case, this priority dictates insight about ourselves and then treating ourselves with respect and good care, even if it means sacrificing a lesser need for excitement and stimulation.

Physical Comfort and Convenience

This one varies enormously. Yet it is amazing how a person who values comfort highly may decide on a spouse who couldn't care less, and who loves vacations in the woods, and work that guarantees discomfort. Of course, all hell breaks loose. The situation or relationship becomes a lost cause, or considerable depression ensues.

Change to a lower position on the scale is rare, so let the people who assign high priority to comfort be wary in decisions they make regarding almost all areas of daily living.

I remember a man whose wife convinced him that he would get used to commuting to work from the suburbs. She loved the country, and roughing it did not bother her at all. He loved comforts of all kinds and really hated to be inconvenienced in any way at all. Waiting for trains, traveling long distances, worrying about schedules, dealing with snow and rain, were monsters he had never dreamed he would encounter. The commute "worked" for about a year. Then a period of anxiety and depression ensued. This was followed by rage and a divorce.

Integrity

This is not a top priority for most people. Of course, here too a question of degree prevails. Most of us are honest most of the time. But most of us idealize ourselves and believe we are more honest than we actually are.

However, there are people for whom these qualities have extremely high priority. Their actual honesty may not be perfect, but these people cannot sacrifice principle for friendship or any other reason, however much devotion they may have for a particular person or cause. They are often scrupulous to a fault. If they are forced into "decisions" that ignore their need for integrity, they usually suffer severe repercussions in the form of self-hate.

Most people with this priority know that they've got it. It seldom remains unconscious, though it often throws them into conflict, since many situations come up in life where compromise is more in demand than integrity.

Others may see making decisions on the basis of this priority as inappropriate rigidity. But decisions based on this priority will actually cause less difficulty to such people in the form of self-rejection and anxiety than decisions that ignore it.

Quality of Time

The productive use of time has absolutely top priority for me. From my point of view, the time of our lives is limited and has more value than almost anything else. When it is over, it is over; I believe in my own mortality. I have enormous interest in and respect for the seconds and minutes of my life. I am well aware of how much can be done in work or leisure or for fun in a single hour. I am also aware that many decisions need time for development and clarity. In decisions that necessitate choice between taking time and paying money, I gladly pay money. Among money, power, prestige and time, there is no contest at all for me. Compared to time, the others are not even in the running. This does not mean I'm in a hurry. Leisure takes time and leisure is important to me. But I try not to waste time.

Spending time frivolously—spending it with people one doesn't like, or doing things one dislikes in order to be liked by people—is to be avoided by anyone to whom the quality of time is precious.

There are people for whom time registers only midscale, and still others who don't care about it at all and live accordingly. There is no right or wrong here. Each stand makes for a different life-style. But again, it *is* wrong not to know where we stand, because our use of time invariably affects decisions about work and relationships to such a large degree.

Weather

I have noticed that the value of weather seems to be a priority of considerable importance among creative people, who are particularly sensitive and vulnerable to surroundings.

High priority about weather can affect decisions about where to live, work, play and vacation, and with whom. A partner who loves other weather or another climate may not be a happy one. This can make for considerable stress, which may have both emotional and physical repercussions. I know a woman who gets depressed when cold weather arrives. Psychotherapy has helped her in many other matters, but her fear and hatred of intense cold persists. Though I have no proof, I believe she has a marked physiological response to weather, since she not only feels much happer during warm weather but is also 95 percent more productive in the summer. Weather, of course, has always been a top priority for her. But her husband insists on their living in the northernmost section of the country, where he grew up. The strain on their relationship every winter is considerable.

This priority is not a minor, superficial or inconsequential one at all: I have known people who have been unhappy and unsuccessful all their lives because they ignored it.

The important thing here, as in all decisions, is: Know yourself, and your decisions will be more realistic and produce greater happiness.

Exploring Feelings About Priorities: Some Predecision Considerations

*B*efore I close this chapter on priorities, let me give you an example of someone who knows how to use his scale of priorities, a friend of mind named Jack Cohen.

Jack lives in New York, on the Upper East Side of Manhattan. The summer before last, his daughter Karen, who is now in law school in California, started an internship in a San Francisco law firm and needed a car to commute between her school and her job. She needed it quickly, so Jack made the decision to send her his car. He gave it to her boyfriend to drive across the country to her, and then sat down to think about what kind of new car he should get.

Jack was already in touch with some of his feelings about the new car he was now planning to buy. The process of deciding to give Karen his car had activated his "prioritizing" machinery. For although Jack had not particularly thought about buying a car before Karen's emergency, the act of making a "command" or emergency decision helped to concentrate his attention on the feelings surrounding the subject of a new car. (The decision process itself always stimulates our awareness of feelings and tends to promote further decision-making.)

The fact that Jack already had some feelings about the new car told him that he had probably been thinking about one, at least as a possibility, on an unconscious level for a while. (Just in case you're wondering how Jack knows so much about his feelings, I should tell you that some time ago he spent several years in psychoanalysis.)

Jack was aware that in ruminating about the kind of car he might like, he was actually triggering the decision process. In fact, as I will point out again when we examine the specific stages of decision-making, no stage of this process is easily separable from the others. In this initial exploration of his feelings, Jack was setting in motion a process that would soon get under way in earnest. Right now, however, his main intention was to bring his feelings around the subject of a new car to the forefront of his conscious mind, where he could have access to them.

Here's how Jack Cohen lined up his priorities in his mind:

1. The first feeling that arose around the issue of a new car was *a strong wish to sustain a state of mental peace.*

This is a top priority with Jack, so naturally, in this context, it occurred to him right away.

Next to the universal issues of human existence—physical survival, family, sex, money, and the rest—Jack rates peace of mind as being supremely important in his life. Partly, this is just because he enjoys feeling good. Partly, it's because he rates *freedom from anxiety* very high. (Years ago, Jack was a very compulsive, self-hating man and a stimulation addict who suffered from bouts of depression and anxiety; this was why he went into psychotherapy.) Finally, peace of mind is high on Jack's priority scale because several years ago he had a mild heart attack. *Freedom from unnecessary stress* is therefore also a main consideration.

(Interestingly, Jack's wife, Helen, would rate *excitement and stimulation* rather high on her own priority scale. On the other hand, as Jack would point out to us, she was never a stimulation addict.)

2. *Money* is important to Jack as well. He no longer cares too much about accumulating it. But he doesn't want to have to work any harder to get it. (Karen's studies are expensive.) He'd give this one a 3.

He suspects that these first two priorities mean he will not be buying a temperamental, extremely expensive foreign sports car!

3. *Ownership of material things* is fairly high on his scale—maybe a 2. In fact, he has to admit that this is probably the reason he wants a car in the first place, since public transportation where he lives is adequate to his needs, and a private car is a luxury. He has to admit to himself, in all honesty, that he doesn't really *need* a car; the idea of *owning* one again is what appeals to him.

Incidentally, this is a feature of his personality that Jack does not especially like or approve of. In his idealizations of himself, he prefers to imagine that he is a free spirit, a total independent, an ascetic who could abandon luxuries in a moment for life as a beachcomber. However, he knows better than to make a decision on the basis of this idealized version of himself. He recognizes that he must accept what he can't change about his personality. He sighs and gives himself due credit for at least being able to admit his true priorities honestly.

4. Aesthetic appeal, occupies a fairly high spot—about a 4. This is an aspect of *pleasure*, and although Jack tends to shy away these days from excess stimulation and excitement, he loves beautiful things, especially beautiful machinery. The model he picks probably wouldn't be expensive, but its design would be important to him.

5. *Comfort and convenience* are also high, though not as high as ownership—maybe a 3. He'd probably enjoy a big, comfortable American car. But then again, he'd also enjoy a smaller car because it would be easier to park in his neighborhood.

The thought of a big American car gives him a twinge of conscience for a moment. He wonders if he "ought" to lean toward an energy-efficient model. *Integrity* has a fairly normal rating on his scale—about a 5. He is not sure why this feeling has come up: probably not so much because it is important to him as because he knows it will be important to Helen! On her scale, he would guess, moral principles are closer to 3 or 2. He concludes (with some relief) that he doesn't have to consider this question right now, but he knows it is something he and Helen will probably have to discuss when it is time to reach a joint decision on the purchase.

6. *Prestige* also occurs to him, briefly, as a priority. Of course, the right car can bring a good deal of prestige in the eyes of some people, and PPR used to have a high rating on Jack's scale. By now, however, "what people think" has dropped to around 7 on his scale as a result of his psychotherapy. He stays in touch with this feeling before his thoughts move on, just long enough to note that it means less than it used to.

Jack decides that, for the moment, he will put the matter aside. He has initiated the decision process by focusing his feelings on a specific problem, and the process will now continue of its own volition. He also knows that he has enough time to come to a good decision, and that if he "sleeps on it"—lets it proceed naturally and in its own good time—he is more likely to make a successful decision than if he forces himself to come to a premature conclusion.

Having begun the decision process creates a feeling of pleasure and anticipation. He has had enough experience with real decision-making by now to know that he always gets something out of this process: It is satisfying even when the decision itself is difficult or unpleasant. Once started, it gives him a sense of power, inner freedom, and ownership of his own life that no other activity can.

Now that Jack has set the process of coming to a decision in motion with these preliminary reflections, I want to introduce you to the actual stages of decisionmaking.

IV

The Eight Stages of Decision-making

*I*t is very important to understand the actual steps or mechanics we go through in making a decision.

When we have a breakdown or blockage in the process, understanding the difficulty can help in finding a remedy. Some people know they have decision-making difficulties, but few know the process sufficiently well to recognize the stage or steps from which the problem arises.

As you will see, understanding the eight steps not only helps in diagnosing individual blockages and problems; this knowledge can also be used to help break through the inertia of a blockage.

The eight-step process comes into play whenever we make a decision. Sometimes we are conscious of going through some of the steps. Usually we go through all of them or at least many of them without being consciously aware of it. But they are there, regardless of the speed with which we arrive at a decision. It doesn't matter if the decision is made over a period of months, or immediately.

According to the decision and the circumstances, each stage will require a different amount of time, and the steps may not be discernible. This, I believe, is because the different steps of the process take place instantaneously, in intuitive moves. I believe intuition itself is the instant integration of the eight steps on a nonconscious level.

Of course, integration is not possible in impulsive or compulsive moves. Nor can it occur when "decisions" are limited to conditioned, reflex-like habit.

It is important to make the process a conscious one—to become fully aware of and to understand each of the steps comprising it. Let's put the whole process into slow motion.

The Eight Stages of Decision-making

Stage 1: Listing and Observing All the Possibilities, Options or Choices Involved in the Issue

Stage 2: Sustaining a Free Flow of Feelings and Thoughts About Each of the Possible Choices

Stage 3: Observing Thoughts and Feelings About Each of the Options and Applying Those Feelings

Stage 4: Relating Choices to Established Priorities

Stage 5: Designation! Coming to a Conclusion by Designating One Choice and Initiating Discarding Those Not Chosen

Stage 6: Registering the Decision

Stage 7: Investing the Decision with Committed Feelings, Thoughts, Time and Energy and Completing the Elimination of the Unused Options

Stage 8: Translating the Decision into Optimistic Action

Stage 1

Listing and Observing All the Possibilities, Options or Choices Involved in the Issue

This is an extremely important phase of the decision process. The simple fact is that a decision cannot be better than the possibilities offered. This initial step will determine whether or not any possibility is overlooked.

Experience in decision-making often helps. I have known any number of people who thought they had exhausted all possible options and who then went on to find others.

This is also the stage where help by others can be extremely useful, provided they do not inundate the decision-maker. There are people who are particularly creative in finding options. I know one woman with a natural genius for finance who can see ten possibilities in an investment where most business people would see only two or three. I know another woman who in a matter of minutes can provide new plot possibilities for playwrights who are stuck. This kind of outside help or inspiration can be very useful provided (1) we don't neglect our own option list and

(2) we are not impounded with a decision not of our own making.

Time can be very important in this initial stage. Of course, in certain situations there is no time and we must make do with the options we have then and there. But if there is time, creative possibilities must not be cut off "in order to get the decision over with."

Ideally, this is the supercreative, nonjudgmental phase of the process. In essence, it means having the freedom to come up with any and all options. Freedom in this context means freedom from the need to be "smart," "appropriate" or "valid." One can even be outrageous in quest of inventive options.

At this point, judgment (an objective, rational evaluation) should *not* play a role. Judgment does play an important role in making decisions, but in this first stage, it impedes creativity. This is the time for letting it all flow freely, any way at all, so as to reveal as much as possible to ourselves. All options, however ridiculous they may be deemed later on, are at this stage equally worthy of consideration.

Self-acceptance and self-trust help here because they permit us to be free of the need to be cool, collected, in charge, unfoolish, even to ourselves. Taking appropriate time and being at ease as much as possible are always constructive, especially in the first phase of the process.

The greatest difficulties associated with Stage 1 are voiced in these ways: "I feel boxed in"; "I really don't see any options"; "None of the choices I come up with appeal to me."

This is probably due to stringent application of logical judgment at the wrong stage of the process, as well as to exorbitant expectations. These expectations may be traceable to all kinds of perfectionistic needs. Often it's a sign of need for a decision that will provide *instant gratification.* Often, too, people in this bind have been avoiding a decision for years and now want to get it over with at once in order "not to be bothered." But there are no substitutes for time and relaxation at this point.

Just sitting quietly may do it, or taking a relaxed walk or soaking in a warm bath. Surprisingly, thinking about the decision as little as possible or (if possible) not at all frequently produces a breakthrough.

In effect, this means letting the unconscious freely come up with ideas, however unconnected they may seem. People undergoing psychoanalysis do this when they lie on a couch and say whatever comes to mind regardless of apparent appropriateness.

I once had a patient who would seem to be stuck with no options to choose from in business problems he had. But his unconscious provided him with creative possibilities through relaxed free association, and sometimes in dreams. He would periodically wake up with choices he dreamed about which had been unavailable to him when he was fully awake. This man was often "locked in" by too much logic and the inability to "let go." It was very gratifying to see a string of options suddenly break loose to consciousness after a long period of his feeling "stuck with nothing." Of course, they were there all the time and were all of his own making. But he needed time and ease to free them from the bondage of logic.

Paradoxically, this is the stage of decision-making when it is best that indecision reign supreme. What I mean, of course, is that we must, at Stage 1, keep ourselves free of making any precipitous decision before all the choices have been adequately explored. Obviously, this can be quite difficult for some of us who "can't wait for things to develop" and have a history of impulsiveness.

Naturally, people who find choice difficult may not be overjoyed in discovering that they in fact do have options. Options can appear as merely burdensome additions to inner conflict and turmoil. Such people may be so frightened by options that they develop a pathetically stunted list, or no list at all. Those who suffer severely in this way avoid all choices and decisions in an attempt to negate the anxiety of severe conflict. Needless to say, this represents abdication from one's own life and the destruction of real freedom. But I want to stress that people in this bind almost never recognize this in themselves. They just can't understand "why good things never happen to me." Insight in this area and in this enormously important first phase is crucial to resolving the problem. Without adequate options, the possibility of choice is severely damaged.

Stage 2

Sustaining a Free Flow of Feelings and Thoughts About Each of the Possible Choices

*I*n this stage we experience how we feel about each option. Sustaining or holding on to the feelings we have has enormous value. When we live with an option for a while, we eventually get to know whether or not the particular route is a good one to take. Some feelings prove to be very strong. On the other hand, some have such low amplitude that sustaining them cannot occur at all, and that almost always means the option is probably not worth attention. This part of the process focuses only very generally on the relative value of each choice.

The job here—if we approach this part of the process consciously—is not logical analysis or even observation of our feelings and thoughts. We want to simply have our feelings and thoughts and let them come up as they will, much as we let the options manifest themselves in the first place.

Please note that this takes place even when we are not conscious of its happening. But consciousness can aid the process.

Let's return to my friend Jack Cohen and the decision process that was initiated when he decided to send Karen his car.

Jack's original "command decision" was actually composed of several decisions that he made without much awareness. First, it was predicated on the quick decision that Karen needed the car at once and that sending her his own car would be a fast and efficient way to solve the immediate problem. He had also decided his car would be adequate for Karen's needs. Finally, he was buying time to gather options and decide on another car for himself. This series of rapid-fire, semiconscious decisions-before-decisions is typical of command decisions. We make such decisions all the time unawares.

Now, however, Jack had the necessary time to make a fully thought out decision on the basis of his options and priorities. His attention had already begun to focus on the issue of the new car, and the next morning he began Stage 1—exploring and calling to mind the various options available.

Being an experienced decision-maker, he enjoyed this part of the process, which took a good chunk of his morning. The fact that it was Saturday helped, because he was relaxed and could allow his mind to range freely over the options. So did the fact that on Saturdays Helen insisted that he take the family dog out for its morning walk. Though Jack spent much of the morning thinking about his choices in regard to the car, most of what occurred actually came into his mind very rapidly—to be exact, in the fifteen minutes that it took him and the dog to struggle along together to the Metropolitan Museum and back. During this part of the process, a great many choices, options and possibilities arose in his mind—some having to do with what type of transportation he wanted, others with what he could afford and how to finance it. He allowed himself, in fact, to consider, at least for a moment, every single choice he could think of, as long as it had four tires and a steering wheel, and he was fairly inventive about the possibilities—new cars, used cars, American cars, foreign cars, rented cars, chauffeured limousines, you name it. (He even asked himself wistfully, for just a moment, why a New York apartment dweller shouldn't own a camper.) He finally ended up with three general possibilities that he felt he would probably devote most of his attention to (though he did not, at this point, rule anything out), mainly because they seemed affordable:

He could buy a new American car.
He could buy a cheap foreign car.
He could buy a used car.

In the days that followed, Jack, moving on through Stage 2 of the process, let himself simply ruminate about many possibilities, though particularly these three. He didn't try very hard to think about any of them. What came to mind, he figured, would be what he was most interested in. He attempted not to interfere with his thoughts at all. Nevertheless, he was very conscious of the feelings that came up whenever he thought of one of his main options. The idea of a used car actually turned him off. He'd had used cars before—"buying someone else's problems," he thought. Buying a new American car felt a lot better. Solid. Warm. Comfortable. (Expensive!) Buying a cheap foreign car—well, an expensive foreign car would have excitement and interest. But a cheap foreign car felt foreign, unfamiliar, unappealing. (But cheap!)

The process was successful in that a free flow of feelings and thoughts was not impeded by sudden, impulsive acting out that might have been destructive.

Stage 3

Observing Thoughts and Feelings About Each of the Options and Applying Those Feelings

After about a week, Jack found that he was beginning to observe and evaluate all the feelings he was having.

He was inclined to take a very serious note of his conflict around buying a new American car. It meant a considerable outlay of money, and in view of the fact that Karen had another year of college, he felt anxious about such an expenditure. On the other hand, he also had to pay careful attention to the feelings around the idea of a cheap foreign car. He was feeling growing uneasiness about his option. Words like "flimsy," "uncomfortable," and even "unsafe" kept occurring to him. Would saving money in the purchase price and the better gas mileage be worth the price he'd have to pay in going against these strong feelings? This didn't seem to be a decision he would ultimately be happy with. But a used car—in this option, he realized, he was just not interested! He could buy a warranty, but to him, driving a used car felt like using someone else's toothbrush. It was beginning to look, he reflected uneasily, as though he might have to resign himself to deciding between the first two options. He didn't feel this was enough of a choice, somehow.

He explored his feelings about rental and leasing too. These options felt both economical and rather creative—clever of him to think of them! But they also felt depressing. Ownership, Jack knew, was what he liked. Possession or nothing. He wouldn't need to explore this one much further. He knew himself well enough to be sure his feelings were based on a strong personal priority.

Observation of the feelings that came up in Stage 2 is extremely important at the third stage of decision-making. Ruminating of this type is neither mystical nor evidence of indecisiveness; it is a natural and necessary part of the process, and experientially valuable. Some of the options will seem good immediately, others will seem "wrong." Similar previous experiences, feelings and thought associations will play a part here. These will provide valuable information as to how we did, in fact, feel and fare in the same or similar situations and issues. Much that we ascribe to intuition goes on at this point.

This is also an important time to take a good, hard look at the feelings and thoughts we have about each choice, offered, giving them a chance to really register. We apply logical rationale to each choice and to our feelings and thoughts about them. This is the constructive use of *judgment*.

Difficulty in this phase, or avoiding it, largely amounts to rushing to conclusions before feelings reach full fruition. This results in impulsive decisions (which are of course pseudodecisions and which will at best waste time). At worst, these lead to grievous disappointments and being so gun-shy that decision-making may reach a state of paralysis. Learning to be patient and to take one's own feelings seriously is crucial.

Of course, people who have spent their lives erasing their feelings and worrying about other people's opinions before their own are going to have a hard time at this stage of the process.

Unfortunately, there are many people who, having gone through the first two steps, fail to really go through the third. A typical response in this situation is: "I thought of that, but paid no attention to it." This kind of difficulty is usually evidence of poor self-esteem and sometimes of hopelessness. It may be the result of chronic depression on the one hand or simply an immediate lack of optimism about finding a suitable decision for the problem.

Having thoughts and feelings is useless if we discard them or trivialize them by adequate attention. The psychoanalyst takes the patient's thoughts and feelings seriously because he takes the patient, himself, and his work seriously. I'm afraid there are a great many people who simply do not take their own feelings about anything seriously enough and this affects this stage of decision-making. Being unable to live with certain choices, however rational and practical they seem, is common. This is avoidable if we give serious attention to how we feel.

Jack had not ruled out the possibility of other options emerging from all the thinking he was doing. He felt this was especially important because he was in conflict about what appeared, at the moment, to be the two likeliest choices he had. He decided to take another look at the feelings, around other possibilities.

How about walking?

Ridiculous.

Well, maybe not so ridiculous, he thought. Maybe not replacing his car was an option he should consider seriously.

Feeling a little foolish, he asked himself what he thought about walking and discovered that he kind of liked the idea.

Cheaper than owning a car. Interesting: See the city the way you never can from inside a car.

But being deprived of his own car? Ouch! And giving up a car to take public transportation? Jack thought of the New York subways, which he tended to avoid. This could be an even bigger ouch!

Taxicabs. Now *that* thought gave him a sense of freedom. They were always available on the streets of New York. You could generally flag one down, or you could order one by telephone. He didn't need a car to commute. He thought of how expensive garage space was in New York and recalled with a sense of outrage the many dents garage attendants had inflicted on his cars in the past. He also thought of the time and aggravation spent on looking for nonexistent street parking, and the fines he had paid in parking tickets. Hm. Maybe the combination of walking and taxicabs wasn't such a dumb idea at all. He felt kind of good about it.

He continued to feel kind of good about it. He also continued to want a big American car all his own. He also continued to wish they cost less, and he kept on disliking the idea of settling for a cheap foreign car.

Jack decided the time had come to figure out what his priorities were.

By now, Stage 3 has been completed; observation leading to logical application has taken place.

Stage 4

Relating Choices to Established Priorities

All areas, issues and items in life occupy different positions of importance for each of us. Some of us are in touch with our priorities, some of us are not. Some of us are alienated from feelings in some areas but not others. This separation from how we feel can vary from one time to another, but our degree of emotional health will dictate how much we are in touch with our feelings.

Those of us who have difficulty with this will experience problems in implementing the fourth step in decision-making. On the other hand, someone who knows the score about his or her priorities has already won half the battle.

Jack had, of course, already done some thinking about this, although not in regard to specific options. He had three choices he was seriously considering and a number of general issues on his priority list that would apply to these choices. Now he was in a position to put his choices together with his priorities and start coming to an actual decision. In this part of the decision process, he decided to be methodical. In fact, about five days after he first started thinking about the car problem, he sat down at his desk with a pencil and a piece of paper and actually jotted down the priorities that applied, so that he could consider them more clearly.

1. *Money.* This might not be an absolute top-priority item in general for Jack—if you remember, he gave it a 3 in his predecision ruminating—but it was a major concern in the purchase, so he gave it a 2. No question that walking and taxicabs would be better than buying any kind of car as far as this priority went. Even if he rented a car every time he went out of town, or took a cab every single time he went anywhere, this option was still the economical one.

2. *Ownership.* He might not like this trait of his, but ownership was still a top priority—a 2. Only buying a car could satisfy this one, and if he didn't own one, he would have to resign himself to feeling fairly deprived.

3. *Prestige.* Less important—still a 6 or 7 in Jack's life in general—but with respect to a car, closely tied in with ownership. He cared less about what people would say about his not owning a car anymore (assuming they cared at all!) than about feeling deprived of ownership itself. But he had always had a car, and it did make him slightly uneasy to think of being someone who other people knew didn't have one.

4. *Pleasure and the aesthetic appeal of a car.* This was, and remained, about a 4 on Jack's scale. He would enjoy having a good-looking car—he even liked the designs of some of the cheaper imports. This one spoke in favor of purchase, though it didn't tell him whether to buy American or foreign.

5. *Comfort and convenience.* Well, this depended on how you looked at it. Getting a taxi could be a nuisance. But parking and servicing a big, comfortable American car was a nuisance too. Either way, this priority was still a 3.

6. *Integrity and moral principle.* Not really an issue, since this was only about a 5 for Jack generally, but he could feel virtuous if he didn't buy a car at all [oil conservation, diminish pollution]. (Helen, he knew, would probably like the idea of *not* buying a car.)

7. *Peace of mind.* Jack put this down last and regarded it soberly. He had to admit that it was still number one with him.

Ownership of a car meant a lot of stress—the maintenance, the financial outlay, and most of all the driving itself, if he drove in town. Of course, there was stress involved in having to look for transportation every time you went anywhere. But when you rented a car or hired a cabbie, you only *rented* aggravation; when you owned a car, you owned that too.

What it came down to for him, he decided, was Ownership versus Peace of Mind.

The money was important, he knew that, but he also knew that it was not as important to him, especially in this case, as ownership, possessing his own car. He would be happy if he saved the money, but he could also afford to spend it, and whether he spent less on a foreign car or more on an American car didn't matter too much; he could afford a car if he really wanted one. The true issue was whether he wanted to buy any car in order to own one, or whether he wanted to give himself a chance—say, a year—to see whether the freedom from stress he could have from relying on his own two feet—plus a corps of New York cabbies— compensated for the deprivation of no longer being the proud possessor of his own car.

There was a lot of inner peace to be had from not owning a car, he reflected.

He thought about this for a few more minutes, then put away his list.

He continued to mull over his options. He continued to

walk around and hail cabs when he needed them. He continued to feel slightly deprived at not having a car while he was coming to his decision.

One day while he was walking downtown, he looked in a Cadillac dealer's show window and realized, with a feeling of mild surprise, that he had made his decision.

Stage 5

Designation! Coming to a Conclusion by Designating One Choice and Initiating Discarding Those Not Chosen

*T*his stage is arrived at smoothly from the preceding stages and especially the latter one. It is the moment when we arrive at a favored option and decide that this is the one we will go with. We designate it as our choice—our only choice, the one we are truly committed to carrying out.

The transition to the Designation stage is almost always imperceptible; most often the choice seems to sneak up on us, before we even realize that we have come to a decision. This is as it should be. If the transition to Designation is contrived and forced, we are usually dealing with a block to the process. Designation makes itself known mainly by the way we feel about it. There is a sense of "things falling together"; the designation of a choice we are committing ourselves to makes us feel "solid" and good about ourselves. This comes from the feeling of knowing ourselves and what we want. It strengthens our confidence in ourselves and strengthens our identity.

But the most important part of this stage, if the decision is a real one, is initiated immediately *after* Designation. I speak now of beginning to discard the unused options so as to clear the way for the designated choice. I'll say more about this process of elimination in describing Stage 7, by the end of which the discards should be out of the way.

Jack had decided to walk. He looked at the display of cars in the Cadillac showroom and another thought drifted into his mind: I'll give it a year.

With pleasure and a mild sense of relief, Jack realized that he had settled on a choice. He had committed himself to a state of easy-going relaxation for a single year. This would give him a chance to find out whether the rewards in terms of freedom from stress—and to a lesser degree, money—really outweighed the satisfaction of owning a good-looking piece of machinery and the convenience of having his own transportation. He didn't have to stick with it for *longer* than a year, but he was willing to commit that much time to finding out what suited him.

Maybe it was silly, but he was kind of proud of himself for having thought of this option. It was the only logical thing to do, he felt. Things had just sort of fallen in place. In fact, at the moment he didn't even *want* to own a car—he was excited about trying out his idea. (He had a flash picture of himself striding commandingly along the streets of the city, hailing cabs that stopped obligingly whenever he beckoned; maybe taking Helen out for a weekend spin in the country in a rented Mazda—no, a Porsche!)

Suddenly he felt absolutely certain that he could live without owning a car—for a year, or even much longer.

Jack congratulated himself. He couldn't explain why, but he felt that settling this problem made him feel bigger than he had been a moment earlier. He had this sense of knowing who he was and what he wanted out of life that went much beyond the immediate issue of transportation. He felt *solid*.

He turned away from the show window and went home happily to talk over his terrific idea with Helen.

Stage 6

Registering the Decision

*T*his is a continuation of the simple act of expressing the choice openly. Jack began this process for himself when he went home "to talk over his terrific idea with Helen."

This meant nothing more than sitting with it for a while; feeling it out; letting it register and sink in and become part of himself.

While we are absorbing the choice we made, we are, if necessary, also still completing the previous stage, the discarding process. We are letting any existing residuals of discarded options drift away. We are saying a definitive goodbye to them even as we are getting closer to and more solid with the choice we *have* made. In effect, we are "getting it all together" in preparation for action.

By the end of this stage and the beginning of the next, buying a car was no longer in Jack's mind.

This is not a testing stage to "see how it feels" in order to backtrack. People who cannot make decisions because of obsessive ruminating usually have their major difficulty at this point. They will prolong this stage way beyond practical need or value. They will sit and sit until their apathy converts the process into a frozen stalemate so that choice never becomes real decision. Characteristically, obsessive ruminators will at this point return repeatedly to Stage 3—observing their thoughts and feelings, reopening this step again and again—and applying "more logic" ad nauseam.

Giving ourselves a real chance to absorb and register the choice helps to complete the discarding process and thus to prepare ourselves for total investment in the decision which is a vital part of decision-making as a whole.

Stage 7

***Investing the Decision with Committed
Feelings, Thoughts, Time and Energy and
Completing the Elimination of
the Unused Options***

*T*his is the stage of commitment in the decision-making
process.

Choice has in effect become decision in the previous
stage. Commitment of ourselves to our choice through the
last two steps completes the transition.

People who make choices for all the wrong reasons—
coercion, to be liked by others, because "it's the right thing
to do," or for purely conventional reasons—will often demonstrate difficulty at this point. They will drag their feet.
They will look back. They will often postpone indefinitely
until "the decision" loses viability or meaning. This eventually is corrosive to morale and establishes a pessimistic
mood antithetical to good decision-making.

Choice is not decision, as far as I'm concerned, unless
implementation takes place. Choice must be translated into
action or inaction—whatever change in status quo is called
for, within a suitable period of time—in order to become a
decision. *This consists of finally and completely eliminating*

the nonchosen options. Surrendering them. Letting them go—all but the ones we have chosen. This *is* making the choice!

Discarding unused choices is what choice is all about, after all. It is what growing up is all about: letting rejected choices go and thus establishing priorities and demonstrating a willingess to pay a price—the price of discarded options—and to take responsibility through our decisions for who we are and what we want.

Discarding other choices has more than one practical purpose; it also withdraws time and energy from the nonchosen options so that we can focus on the chosen ones.

This is the stage that establishes focus of time, energy, self and purpose. If the stage is fully successful, there is no fragment of self left looking back at residual possibilities. There are no regrets for discards! Focus on the choice, which is now very rapidly maturing into decision, brings a high concentration of ourselves, which is characteristic of unified purpose.

The most common problem in this stage is wanting it all. Thus, if we realize that indecision is sustained because we cannot surrender the unchosen options, we will know that our difficulty occurred at the fifth through the seventh step.

At this point, the stage is set for going on with conversation from choice to action. Stage 7 acts as the final bridge between choice and decision; between the potential and the kinetic; between thought and action. This is where we cross the Rubicon.

We have made a decision. Now we demonstrate that we are truly committed to our choice.

Stage 8

Translating the Decision into Optimistic Action

*T*his last stage could well be called "Loyalty and Optimism," because that is what is is all about.

We are not rigidly locked into any decision. *Appropriate* change is desirable. But this possibility must not in any way hamper or dilute continuing loyalty to decisions made.

This is the phase in which we help ourselves in every way possible to *make it work!* Though another decision might have turned out equally well, we are loyal and optimistic about this one. *This one* is the one that is ours *at this time.* Its being *ours* is reason enough to give it all we've got, in the mood of optimism and utter loyalty that is characteristic of successful enterprise.

People who suffer from self-hate have a great deal of difficulty sustaining either loyalty or optimism in decision-making or in any matter that involves themselves. They tend to abandon decisions at any sign of difficulty and quickly become pessimistic about the wisdom and outcome of their choices. There are a number of people with poor self-esteem who go through the first seven steps of the process fairly well but who fail in the final stage, when the inevitable bump in the road presents itself.

My friend Jack had enough self-esteem to begin investing his decision with loyalty and optimism right away. He began doing this virtually from the moment he made his choice, when in his mind's eye he optimistically pictured himself carrying out the decision. He invested it with more loyalty and optimism when he went off to enlist Helen's support, and again when he gave over a full morning to check out taxi and car services.

He kept on giving it his loyalty and optimism. Inevitably, there were times when he got mad at the decision—like the following winter when he and Helen had to wait twenty minutes on a cold street corner for a taxi that never arrived, and missed the first act of a Broadway show they'd paid eighty dollars to see. And inevitably, there were moments when he would pass the Cadillac showroom and think wistfully of owning a car again. But he reminded himself that even if he didn't own a car, he owned a commitment to a choice—*his* choice, the only one at this time. He could always get a car after a year or more if his desire to have one was still strong. Jack stuck by his decision.

As a matter of fact, Jack and Helen did finally get a car again, about fourteen months after the original decision. But because Jack was loyal to himself and optimistic that choosing to do without a car for a year would tell him how much he really wanted one, he found out what he wanted to know. So the decision—and the entire experience—was a success and contributed to his self-growth and maturity.

A Few More Words

*J*ack's decision was successful for a number of reasons.

First, he knew from the start that *real decisions are possible only when we know what we feel.* He was at all times in touch with his real feelings and the values and priorities that sprang from them—even when he didn't like or feel completely comfortable with those feelings.

Second, he understood all along that *the process of coming to a real decision is a healthy and satisfying one,* which produces a sense of growth and accomplishment. He was willing to give the process all he needed to give in terms of energy, time, thought and feelings in order to make the decision a good one. And he knew that *the process is a creative one,* which promotes success in the future. *Successful experience with the decision process itself is the best way to become a successful decision-maker.*

Third, Jack permitted full confidence in himself and his decision. He invested the choice he made with commitment and hope. He did not permit self-hating idealization (for instance, the wish to see himself as "free" of the desire for ownership) to sidetrack the process at any point. And he let himself continue to believe in and carry out the choice he had made in spite of temporary setbacks.

And finally, he knew that no matter what choice he actually made, the Big Fact was on his side. Any choice he made would be a constructive one, as long as it sprang from his real desires, values and priorities, and had his full commitment.

But what if someone—even a fairly healthy, fairly success-ful decision-maker like Jack Cohen—can't come to a decision? What happens if we get deadlocked at some point in the decision process? This can happen even to experi-enced decision-makers, and this is what I want to consider next.

V

Breaking Deadlocks

*Breaking Out
of Deadlocks*

Sometimes decision deadlocks occur no matter what we do or how hard we try. "I just go up and back and can't come to a decision."

Usually people can work their way out of impasse puzzles. (This, of course, means knowing that a puzzle exists, which is not always true of people severely removed from their feelings.) Of course, motivation is invaluable, as is the desire for better living. Working our way out of impasses provides hope and optimism. Both these qualities, at least in modest amounts, are necessary for constructive, healthy change and growth to take place in all areas, including this one.

In this chapter I review and discuss some aids, should an impasse occur.

Breaking Out of Deadlocks

1. Rest

2. Accept Imperfection

3. Remember the Big Fact!

4. Free Association

5. Rest Again, and Boost Morale

6. The Eight Stages

7. Review Priorities

8. Blockages Again

9. Pride Stands and Pride Teases

10. Outside Help.

1. Rest

Have you tried to put the whole thing aside for a while and get some really distracting rest from it? Ease your mind and give it a chance to get into good shape again. Sleep, dinner, a walk, movies, friends, work (for some people), helping someone else, playing catch, calisthenics, dancing—to each his own. Any enjoyable distraction is good. Don't worry; the problem and the opportunity to resolve it will still be there when you get back.

So if you can, abandon it for a while and give yourself a chance to regroup and replenish. This sometimes helps to develop a fresh and even a new outlook. I like to relax in a warm bath for a long time.

It is important at this point to remind yourself that *you* come first, before anything or anyone, and before the decision itself. However any decision comes out, your survival and well-being are always of primary importance.

It is of value to tell yourself in so many words again and again that you yourself are more important than any issue under consideration. Let this sink in! Being convinced of this fact has great ameliorative power for your well-being generally, and also for the decision-making process itself.

2. Accept Imperfection

You must at this point make sure that you truly know that all things in life are imperfect. I spoke of this in our discussion of blockages. Decisions are always imperfect!

So many deadlocks are due to the wish to make a 'perfect' decision that I want to stress here again that only death is perfect. When you embrace imperfection you embrace life, and you enhance yourself. Exorbitant expectations hurt us and are death to decision-making. You will be doing fine if the choice you make is free of any coercion and reflects your own feelings and priorities.

3. Remember the Big Fact!

Recall it at least several times. Say it out loud: *In very few instances is one decision actually better than another.* We must give up a number of choices, quit them, let them go, in order to invest ourselves in the choice or choices we make.

The choice will become a good decision if we can dedicate ourselves to making it a good one!

---

4. Free Association

Free associate. Let your mind bring up anything at all that's even remotely connected to the issue. Suspend judgment, criticism or logic as much as you can. This is a loosening-up exercise as well as a way to generate options. It will help relax you and free you to get in touch with your real feelings—especially those that may be keeping you in a state of conflict and paralysis.

---

5. Rest Again, and Boost Morale

If no chance has occurred and nothing has come up, make the decision to make no decision for a while. Rest again and do everything possible to boost your morale. Go out and do anything that is uplifting and feels good.

You and your mind are one and the same. Taking care of yourself through increasing a mood of optimism and well-being replenishes and tunes up your mind.

---

6. The Eight Stages

If there is still no breakthrough, go over the *eight-stage decision process* carefully. Apply each stage to the issue and put them all down on paper from Stage 1, listing all the options right through to action. Going through the stages often results in a breakthrough.

7. Review Priorities

Now, if necessary, go over your priorities again and make whatever connections there may be between them and the issue at hand.

Going over priorities can be very helpful in breaking a decision deadlock. The choice may actually come down to two options that pull absolutely equal weight. Perhaps you've determined, for instance, that freedom from stress is of very high priority to you. At this point you may realize that one option will bring less stress than the other and feel that this one is clearly your designated choice—the one that best fits this priority.

8. Blockages Again

But let's say you still can't do it. Another rest may be valuable. Refresh yourself as much as possible and then get down to some diagnostic work. Go over the blockages again—the whole list if necessary. Try to locate the culprit. Find the one in operation and apply your insight. Give it all you've got to take a chance and to break through!

9. Pride Stands and Pride Teases

What if there is still no breakthrough? You may be caught in a "pride stand." Neurotic pride does terrible things to us. We do the most destructive things to ourselves in order to sustain our proud, idealized images or inflated versions of ourselves. We get caught in pride stands this way so that even though we know which choice is good for us, we won't move because the reality choice may detract from our self-glorifying trip.

A "pride tease" is an offshoot of a pride stand, the habitual self-inflating operation. In a pride tease, a choice is offered that in some way inflates us even though it is bad for us. We know we must not accept it, but we can't turn it down.

Knowing the difference between real desire for self-realization and pride teases that support unreal versions of self can help break through a deadlock. Pride teases are almost always connected to what other people will think: "*They* will love me." "*They* will admire me." This leads to momentary feelings of self-inflation, and these feelings make us very vulnerable to outside influence, including all kinds of cultural dicta about what we ought to earn, look like, smell like, etc.

Real desire is based on what is really good for us rather than the image. It springs from the self and gives self-satisfaction rather than heavy reliance on outside motivation, support or rewards.

Years ago, before I knew any of this, I was offered an opportunity to teach a rather technical course. I knew that the course did not interest me. But I was told that I would be the youngest man in the school ever to have taught the course. The pride tease hook was in. I could not make a decision. I sweated over it past the deadline. The faculty finally made my pseudodecision for me and committed me to it. I spent a whole summer preparing for the course and then six months teaching it. I hated all of it.

The fact is, the pride boost it gave me was over before I even started to teach. It did not enhance my real self a bit. I missed out on things I really wanted to do. I can assure you that I've been very careful of pride teases ever since!

10. Outside Help

There are people in whom deep resignation or removal from feelings is profound enough to require help. Help, however, *does not mean someone else making decisions for troubled individuals*. Help means helping them to know the difference between image and self. It means helping them to get over the unhealthy need for self-inflation. It means helping them to revitalize their feelings and their values and helping them to know themselves. It means helping them to analyze their decision problems and to support *their own decisions*.

The "Point Logic" Method

*L*et us say you are still in a heavy bind. This can happen to anyone—one doesn't have to be especially neurotic. There are issues for everyone that are particularly sticky.

Here is a "point logic" method to be used if all other efforts have failed. I emphasize that this method is for use only if absolutely necessary, because it does not add greatly to sustained growth in decision-making. However, it is helpful in an emergency.

What we do is simply to take the deadlock and construct a mechanized point system based on priorities and issues relevant to the case. We then add up the points and go with the larger sum. Here's an example:

Let's say I can't choose between buying a house in the suburbs or staying in the city. I've worked and worked on it and no decision is forthcoming. I'm stuck!

I assign from 1 to 10 points to issues involved in this deadlock, in accordance with my own priorities.

Fresh air. Important but not urgent. 4 points.

Quiet. Some relevance but not extremely important. 2 points.

Convenience and freedom from stress. Great importance for me. 10 points.

Stimulating environment. Moderate importance. 5 points.

Economic considerations (saving money). A bit more than moderate. 6 points.

Aesthetics. Moderate. 4 points.

Room (spaciousness). Number of rooms and square footage are important. 7 points.

Time. Very important indeed. 10 points.

Now I evaluate each option in terms of points given to each priority. Most are obvious.

Priority	City	Suburbs	Comment
Air	0	4	The city loses here.
Quiet	0	2	The city busts out here.
Convenience and freedom from stress	10	0	The city wins with this one because of commuter stress.
Stimulation	5	0	The city is more stimulating!
Economy	6	6	A draw. Rent cheaper in suburbs but balanced by cost of commute.
Aesthetics	0	4	Some people like tall buildings. No beauty in it for me.
Room	0	7	Country houses are bigger than city apartments.
Time	10	0	Again, the commuting factor.
Points:	31	23	

I decide in favor of the city and I go with my decision all the way so that eventually my feelings will catch up to my logic.

Now you may ask, what happens if it is a dead heat? I toss a coin and I go with the results! I move accordingly and I am loyal to my decision and to myself. If I understand the decision process, the Big Fact and the fact that commitment indicates compassion for myself, ambivalent feelings will soon dissipate. I proceed to live!

VI

The Twenty Secrets of Decision Success

Actually, these aren't "secrets" at all. Or if they are, this is only because we keep them secret from ourselves.

What I call the Twenty Secrets or Twenty Essentials of Decision Success are the *attitudes we must cultivate to achieve our goals in all areas of life*—not just before, during and after making a specific decision, *but all the time*.

These attitudes are indispensable to making a decision work. But they are much more than just that. Just as the decision blockers are the great enemies of success and happiness, these are the great promoters of success and happiness in all aspects of life. Knowing and *using* them—putting them into practice in every area of endeavor—is essential for full self-ownership and self-realization.

Although they are numbered, I have not arranged them in any special order of importance. They are all important! Like the decision blockers, they overlap and feed each other—but in a constructive way, not a destructive one. In fact, you will probably be able to anticipate many of them just from what I've said about the blockages. As a group, the Twenty form a dynamic, health-promoting "system" of their own—the antithesis of and antidote to abdication and self-defeat. When applied and practiced repeatedly, they actually help to dissolve inhibiting blockages. And wherever they coexist in our lives, they reinforce and strengthen each other, extending and perpetuating their benevolent influence in every branch of existence.

The Twenty Secrets or Essentials
of Decision Success

1. Knowing Your Priorities

2. Establishing Realistic Goals and Expectations

3. Knowing There Is Always a Price to Pay

4. Self-Confidence I: Recognizing Major Personal Assets

5. Knowing and Exploring Your Proclivities

6. Self-Confidence II: Getting Over Fear of Rejection and Failure

7. Knowing That It Is Easier to Leave a Person, Place, Situation, Job, Activity or Anything Else than to Find One to Go To.

8. Knowing That Conditions Are Always Imperfect

9. Recognizing That Moods Make a Difference

10. Accepting Ambivalence

11. Self-Confidence III: Handling Insecurity and Anxiety

12. Acquiring Commitment, Investment, Involvement

13. The Value of Integrated Concentration

14. Profiting from Other People's Experience, Expertise and Help

15. Delegating Responsibility

16. The Effective Use of Time

17. Insight, Motivation, Discipline

18. The Postponement of Gratification

1. Knowing Your Priorities

*W*e've already talked a great deal about priorities. But I want to stress a few points here. Prioritizing is, after all, an essential prerequisite for success.

You already know that establishing priorities is in itself an exercise in choice and in self-assertion. Each time we announce a priority, we state a personal preference—we are choosing. But the reverse is also true. Each time we make a decision or assert ourselves, we are prioritizing.

Continuing to decide and act in terms of priorities is an exercise necessary for the maintenance of organization of our resources. We become integrated—"together." We perpetuate our "togetherness" by continuing to prioritize in all the different areas of our lives.

As decisions based on priorities are practiced, we become more skillful at focussing ourselves on the attainment of goals and self-fulfillment. Priorities tell us many things besides who we are: what we want, how to get it, where we want to go, the prices we have to pay, and how to get there. There is little as important to success in any area.

2. Establishing Realistic Goals and Expectations

*W*e cannot get more from life on this planet than life on this planet has to offer.

Appropriate or realistic expectations prevent grievous disappointments. They prevent achievements and attainments from turning to ashes as soon as we have them. They prevent insatiability, chronic hunger and the what-has-life-done-for-me-lately syndrome. They prevent future inertia and resignation.

In *Compassion and Self-Hate*, I said: "The process is the product." This statement means that if *doing*—that is, the actual process of getting to the goal—is satisfying, attainment of the goal does not have to produce cataclysmic results to be satisfying. To the extent that we can sustain maximum enthusiasm even as we keep our expectations reasonable, we will sustain good morale and continue to maintain our commitment.

By the same token, appropriate or realistic goals are success-oriented goals. "Realistic" means the goals are appropriate to our degree of expertise. They spring from solid research that shows they are attainable in the real world. They are based on real decisions.

The success that realistic goals bring builds self-esteem and good morale, which contribute to the habit of success and more ambitious (but still realistic) goals.

Goals that are based unrealistically on poor information, self-inflation, pride, poor research, very limited experience, or no expertise are designed for failure. And failure is often a habit.

To break the habit, it is wise at first to choose simple goals, easily attainable so as to make success an odds-on favorite. This is especially valuable early on in teaching young children, in whom these success-promoting attitudes will become firmly ingrained, lifelong habits.

3. Knowing There Is Always a Price to Pay

You already know that choice leading to a decision costs the options we did not choose—the discards. This principle applies to *all* actions—and to inaction as well.

Show me an action and I'll show you a price! The price we choose to pay is directly related to our priorities and to the decisions we make. There are no exceptions. A price must be paid if a decision is made, if a decision is not made, and no matter what decision is made.

Unwillingness to pay a price destroys the possibility of decision, responsible action and success. Denial of this reality blocks maturity and contributes to chronic, childish yearning for what cannot be. Even the most satisfying outcome has its limitations and cannot provide perfect comprehensive solutions. On the other hand, to try to make a decision or to get what we want without payment produces paralysis and stultification.

But knowing that a price must be paid makes satisfaction (in human proportion) possible. Knowing and accepting the price and the fact that it must be paid actually liberates us. If we recognize the fact that all choice requires discards and all action involves paying a price for achieving a goal, we are free to give up paralysis and the child's wish to have it all.

Human existence has built-in limitations. But when we freely, with fully conscious awareness, choose and take responsibility for the price we pay and know what we want in return we can make real decisions, assert self-ownership, and greatly increase our chances of success.

4. Self-Confidence I: Recognizing Major Personal Assets

*S*elf-confidence makes all the difference—not just in coming to a choice but in the successful carrying out of the decision. Without self-confidence, belief and commitment to a decision are impossible. Our decisions are us, and if we do not have belief in ourselves, we will be uncommitted to our decisions. But with self-confidence—which comes from self-esteem—extraordinary (though not unlimited!) achievements are possible.

I have said a great deal about self-esteem under Global Block 4 in the chapter on the decision blockers. If self-esteem is poor and self-confidence is low, dissolution of this block may require getting to the underlying causes. Psychotherapy may in fact be advisable if this is the case.

Nevertheless, self-confidence can often be strengthened—not superficially but genuinely strengthened—when we recognize consciously that *we have more assets than we may realize*. The trouble is, too many of us have lost touch with what constitute "human assets" or "personal assets."

Many of us simply have never known that these are assets at all and just take them for granted. A personal inventory can be helpful here, even for people who could probably benefit from psychotherapy to get at the cause of poor self-esteem.

What follows is a list of personal assets. They are not superficial or trivial. I ask you to read it and apply it seriously. None of us has all these advantages. *But those that we do have are precious. They are genuine assets. They are sources of strength*. As such, they should by no means be minimized. On the contrary, a personal inventory list constitutes a potent weapon against one of the most awesome blocks to decision power and provides a solid, realistic resource for raising self-esteem, now and in the future.

I list the assets in no particular order. Remember, *knowing* that these are assets constitutes a major step on the road to success.

Some Major Personal Assets

- Good physical health, strength and vitality
- Having a family, siblings and friends
- Having had caring and responsible parents
- Having had parents who provided a model of mutual love
- Coming from a life-affirming family that had a capacity for joy
- Coming from a family whose members cooperated with each other
- A family background that permitted free expression of emotions
- Strong gender identification (knowing and feeling like a male or a female)
- Having sexual feelings
- A history of productive functioning

- A pleasant appearance, good looks or unusual attractiveness
- A sense of humor
- Good intellectual endowment
- Imagination and creativity
- Aesthetic appreciation
- Articulateness
- Stick-to-it-iveness *and* flexibility
- Education
- Homemaking skills
- Earning power
- Good judgment
- Teaching ability
- A capacity for new interests
- Strong feelings
- A capacity for involvement with people, activities and causes
- Any kind of charm or charisma
- Any talent or special skills
- Money, especially money you earned
- Liking people
- A history of sexual and emotional exchange
- Frustration tolerance
- Anxiety tolerance
- The ability to be alone
- Healthy desires and ambitions
- Occupational fulfillment
- Being able to discern reality from fiction

5. Knowing and Exploring Your Proclivities

Knowing your talents, assets, abilities and inclinations, as well as your limitations, is obviously of enormous value. But only if these things are not ignored or neglected. I agree with Karen Horney that ignoring inner resources and creative urges has ultimately a terrible corroding effect on identity.

When we know ourselves and explore what we know, the application of effort to that which is already in motion increases efficacy tenfold. Developing our proclivities is one cure for self-idealization and self-delusion.

The nurturing of proclivities is especially important with children. When their true proclivities are ignored, children fail to develop solid identities, self-esteem and the ability to enjoy healthy activity. We simply must not ignore urges, or even mere inclinations, in children—to write, to paint, to rhyme, to chatter, to read.

For that matter, we must not ignore them in our adult

selves. The need to converse, the yen to go to open spaces, the hankering to visit an art gallery or write a poem—we must foster all that sustains and replenishes our emotional well-being.

6. Self-Confidence II: Getting Over Fear of Rejection and Failure

*T*he fear of rejection by others and the need for total, unequivocal success every time out comes from self-rejection and fear of self-hate. This stems from the obsessive need for "love" or total acceptance by all others—the major block I described in Chapter 2. This need places our well-being in other people's hands. It makes a mockery of the process of decision-making.

Acceptance of self and getting over fear of rejection puts out well-being into our own hands. Unlike the withholding of commitment, which gives the illusion of independence, self-confidence as the result of self-acceptance and freedom from anxiety about rejection is the real thing. It bestows on us genuine independence; freedom of choice, decisions and movement; and the important freedom to be involved and committed without fear.

I believe that our society brainwashes us into feeling that we must succeed and must be accepted every time we move toward someone or undertake any activity at all. If we fail, we are disgraced. This results in terribly hurt pride, embarrassment, attacks of self-hate, feelings of abuse, and depression when we are rejected.

This fear of rejection results in "decisions" designed to prevent the possibility of failure and rejection: dates never asked for, jobs never applied for, favors shied away from, and on and on. These moves destroy the possibility of success.

The rampant fear of rejection also kills spontaneity and adventurous moves of any kind. It leads to an exaggerated and devoted quest for safety from embarrassment, taking energy away from creative enterprise. Fear of rejection and failure is the opposite of self-confidence and success. It is a self-fulfilling prophecy and a *prescription for failure*. For if we never dare allow ourselves to be rejected or to fail (and who in life does not fail—frequently?), we cut ourselves off from the experience of rejection and failure. We become paralyzed in our anxiety. And paralysis brings further inexperience with rejection and failure, which perpetuates paralysis, which perpetuates inexperience and so on.

There is no easy way for those of us who would liberate ourselves from this bind. We simply must take chances and come to realize that while our pride may be hurt, our real selves remain unscathed.

Allowing oneself to be rejected—actually permitting rejection and gradually becoming inured to it as well as to any so-called failures—is liberating beyond belief. We are then truly free! We then become able to knock on any door, to try many things, to ask, to explore, to be enterprising in all areas of life. We are free to tap any and all of our inner resources. We are free to make decisions—real decisions—not out of fear but out of real desire, secure in the knowledge that no outside rejection or outcome will result in self-rejection or self-hate.

7. Knowing That It Is Easier to Leave a Person, Place, Situation, Job, Activity or Anything Else Than to Find One to Go To

I listen much more carefully to the men and women who tell me where they are going than to those who tell me simply that they are leaving.

Success demands decisions that *lead somewhere*. Abandoning a present position is ineffective without choices that lead *to* places, people and activities. Such choices indicate the responsibility necessary for decision success. *Leaving* is not involving. *Going to* something is involving. Not haphazard quitting and a position of continued detachment, but exploring possibilities for constructive change is necessary.

People who want to leave—leave someplace, someone or something—but can't tell you where they want to go are invariably chronically dissatisfied. They are seldom involved in what they are doing or whom they are doing it with, and have no idea what would involve them. They are often resigned, passive people who suffer from profound inertia and lack of decision-making ability. And their chronic complaining changes nothing!

People who want to leave often have an imaginary place to which they want to go. Real places which do exist come off poorly compared to the imaginary "that place." They never find "that" place or person and never go anywhere, and feel empty and cheated all their lives. If I compare my house to an imaginary dream house, my house comes off poorly and I destroy any chance of enjoying it. On the other hand, if I compare it to houses that actually exist, it may come off well in terms of any *real* specifications a house requires to be comfortable. This is a true luxury, one I can appreciate in reality.

Decisions about leaving without destinations are suspect.

Decisions involving destinations are usually the real thing.

8. Knowing That Conditions Are Always Imperfect

*I*f we make the demand for other demands to go away, we will wait forever. Yes, we need to concentrate. Yes, there are times when outside diversions and commitments make this impossible. Yes, there are times that are absolutely antithetical to decisions, actions, planning, or to change of any kind.

But perfect conditions do not exist. Even so-called right conditions don't usually exist. We must often make them as right as we can and move ahead. There simply is no way to totally control either the environment or conditions. Predictability does not exist and is largely a product of self-delusion. In most situations we must make do with much less than perfect conditions and accomplish what we must with what we've got to accomplish it.

It is imperative that our decisions and moves be predicated on our needs, desires, assets and priorities. It is imperative that we know that success through decision power is the result of commitment to our choice. The conditions in which we take action are relevant to the outcome. But it must be remembered that they are never perfect, and they are usually of secondary importance: *Commitment* is what makes the real difference.

9. Recognizing That Moods Make a Difference

All of us have different moods at different times. This is part of the life process. *Moods affect our decisions.*

Moods change.

The trick as far as decision-making goes is not so much to transcend our moods as to know what they are. We must know them, accept them, and often wait for the *right mood.*

A good mood to make a good decision in, and one in which moves are likely to succeed, is one in which we feel relatively comfortable with ourselves, when morale is relatively high.

Feelings of vindictiveness, depression, euphoria, hopelessness and rage, on the other hand, do not make for good decisions. When these are used to break impasses, they are used destructively.

Of course, we must be wary of procrastination being rationalized by (fabricated) bad moods. But assuming that we are in the process of making a genuine decision, and assuming that it is not a command decision and there is sufficient time, I am all for getting over a bad or painful mood, even if this takes longer than anticipated.

It is important to be aware of any strong or unusual mood when we are making decisions, even if the mood is enjoyable. A couple of months ago, the owner of a restaurant I occasionally go to decided that she was going to redecorate. The restaurant is in a wealthy, rather formal part of the city and the decor of the dining room is simple but elegant. However, while in the process of deciding what fabrics to buy, she took a vacation in Mexico City, where she had such a good time that she came back wildly enthusiastic about Mexican peasant art. She decided to "give the place a new look" and spent a couple of weeks extolling the beauties of adobe walls and pre-Columbian statuettes. Fortunately—in my opinion—the restaurant was reviewed in a local paper right after her return and its "elegant neoclassical decor" was singled out for praise.

My friend sobered up and began to consider whether her euphoric mood was the best state of mind in which to make a significant business decision. She realized rather rapidly that however enjoyable her vacation had been, the change she was contemplating might very well cost her her clientele. She bought herself some handsome Mexican planter boxes for her backyard, and decided to stick to elegant neoclassical decor in her restaurant.

10. Accepting Ambivalence

Moods are usually short-lived. Ambivalence—having mixed feelings—may last. We may give ourselves enough time and still feel ambivalent. But if we wait for a clear-cut feeling about an issue in order to make a decision, we may wait forever.

Not only do human beings feel ambivalent a lot of the time, they have multitudinous feelings at the same time, and sometimes when they don't want them.

We must expect a normal amount of ambivalence. *This is no reason not to move ahead.* If we cannot get ourselves to move ahead because of conflicting feelings, time may be necessary. But be wary here of a major blockage—the unwillingness to pay a price. Consult your hierarchy of priorities.

However, even if lingering doubts persist about the decision made, please realize this is normal and human. It does not constitute evidence of a "wrong" decision. With commitment to a decision, intrusive and distracting feelings and thought usually dissipate fairly soon.

11. Self-Confidence III: Handling Insecurity and Anxiety

*L*ike other conditions for decision-making, *feelings are never perfect*! At best, we nearly always have some feelings of insecurity and anxiety about the decision—before making our choice, and after too.

In fact, the decision-making process itself, as with all potential changes and creative moves, generates some *healthy anxiety*. I suspect that this kind of anxiety is part of the process of alerting us and preparing us for a move and a shift of center of gravity. It is, I think, an aspect of the preparation an actor undergoes before he or she walks on stage, which, to me, is not stage fright. It is a *preparatory anxiety* and is part of the self-mobilizing and awakening process.

In any case, if we wait to be totally secure and anxiety free before making decisions and moves, we will wait till doomsday.

I constantly hear people talk about the things they won't do because they are afraid. There are a great many times when we can decide and carry out goals very successfully even while we are afraid—as long as preparation has been adequately and intelligently made. (I am talking about normal fear and not panic.) Moreover, to the degree that we accept fear and anxiety, they will not be able to snowball. The worst anxiety and fear are due to the process of getting anxious about being anxious and being afraid of being afraid. President Franklin Roosevelt put it beautifully: "The only thing we have to fear is fear itself." If we do not get anxious about being anxious, we stop major anxiety-producing machinery before it starts.

12. Acquiring Commitment, Investment, Involvement

You already know about these three. If any ingredients can guarantee success in decision-making, these can. However, there is one important thing I haven't said that I want to say here, because amazingly few people are aware of this particular "secret."

Interest very often comes *after* involvement.

Putting it another way, interest or investment seldom comes *before* involvement. It's simple: If we don't try something, we will never know if we are interested. Some of us—a lot of us—might have to wait around a hundred years for an interest in something to strike us in order to get involved. But waiting for interest to strike is often a rationalization to sustain resignation. It's another of those round-robin deals. To be successful with a decision, you must be actively involved in carrying it out. To be involved, you must be interested and emotionally invested in it. But involvement is what leads to interest and investment in the first place!

If we help ourselves to get sufficiently involved, we will become skillful at involvement in whatever it is—and enjoy it. This, believe me, will produce a lot of interest—and further successful involvement.

13. The Value of Integrated Concentration

"Integrated concentration" really means bringing our total selves—all our resources, time and energy—into focus on the action at hand, to the exclusion of all other matter. This is a companion to commitment and involvement, and if it accompanies the carrying out of a decision, it is an enormously powerful and effective force.

Divisive thoughts or diversions of any kind distract inner resources and energy from the job at hand and aid the cause of a divided self. Ambivalent feelings usually drift away, but indulging and feeding distractions dilutes concentration and effective effort.

On the other hand, the habit of great concentration accounts for what seem enormous and even fantastic accomplishments. Practicing integrated concentration, to the exclusion of distractions and intrusive thoughts, can produce results most people do not ordinarily know they are capable of.

Furthermore, I believe that the great scientific and artistic geniuses of history—whether Copernicus, Mozart, Darwin, Dostoevsky or Freud—owed their achievements not only to great intellectual and creative gifts but to an extraordinary ability to bring integrated concentration to bear on any project they invested themselves in.

One decision, one action, at a time aids the probability of integrated concentration and concerted activity. When integrated concentration is applied to an issue requiring choice and decision, it aids the whole process enormously. Karate experts bring this kind of concentration to bear when they break heavy boards with a hand chop. Similarly, we can bring great power and efficiency of effort to decisions with full concentration of our total selves.

14. Profiting from Other People's Experience, Expertise and Help

Other people's experience can be enormously helpful. With it we can leapfrog both time and lack of training. But it can only be helpful if it is used.

Most people, mainly because of pride, cannot make use of other people's experience. Many cannot accept expertise or help. Most people cannot even listen to others' advice— or rather they seem to be listening but cannot make use of it.

To learn to listen to, to evaluate, to tap and to use the wisdom of others is an incomparable aid in decision-making and the action that follows. This takes receptivity and is born of humility and a true feeling of self-worth.

Many of us resist use of other people's experience because we are afraid of our own potential dependency and compliancy. To the extent that we can assert ourselves, we can overcome this fear and use other people's expertise (even our parents'), much as we use that of doctors and lawyers.

Interestingly, I find that people who have strong ideas of

their own are least reluctant to make use of expert consultation. However, these are people who are not sensitive to coercion and who are not readily inundated by other people's manipulations.

15. Delegating Responsibility

An enterprise of any consequence is almost always markedly limited if there is inability to delegate. The ability to delegate is limited by lack of trust, the need to exploit, self-idealization and an unhealthy need to show mastery. *Healthy growth of an enterprise is usually directly proportional to good and appropriate delegation.*

The ability to delegate represents an extremely important aspect of cooperation. When asked, "How did you do it so well and so fast?" the answer usually is, "*I* didn't—*we* did."

Many excellent choices are destroyed in the action phase of the decision process because of inhibition in this area.

People who can delegate often do so to individuals who they know can do the job, even if they cannot do it as well as the delegators themselves can. They delegate to people less skilled than themselves because they have enough humility to know they cannot do it *all* themselves. They are also well in touch with their hierarchy of priorities and with the fact that time is limited. They choose what they feel is important for them to do, especially the area of decision-making itself. They simply do not permit themselves to be overwhelmed by the need to do everything. They are usually also unselfishly cognizant of the need for other people to have experience so as to reach a decision-making level.

A patient I had was the head of his own engineering company. He was quite competent and the business expanded over the years. But even though the company was growing and his staff was large and capable, Sam kept all the important or difficult jobs for himself: He simply felt (and he may have been right) that no one could do the job as well as he could, and each job was "too important" to entrust to anyone less skilled. As a result, after several more years, during which his company was unable to fulfill all its contracts, business fell off. This, and a prolonged hospital stay brought on by overwork, finally convinced Sam that he was not superhuman and must relinquish some of the responsibility if his business was to survive. This was difficult at first. But as other and younger people began picking up the work load, the business began to run better too.

16. The Effective Use of Time

As I defined it earlier in this book, *good time* or "quality" time is time used effectively. This includes time for relaxation. *Bad time* is time used for self-corrosion, avoidance, procrastination, and for missing opportunities in the service of self-hate.

We've discussed time in the context of priorities. It took me years to find out that in combination with integrated concentration, an hour is an enormous amount of time. It still amazes me how much can be done in a *solid hour*.

It took me just as long to learn that the realization of complex goals took appropriate time and suffered from being awarded insufficient time.

Evolution of clarification does not happen if time is used badly. The gradual clarification of goals does not happen without our effort—in quality time, time used for integrated concentration.

But time itself does not straighten things out. We straighten things out in our minds—through examination, perception, struggle and research—in a timely fashion.

17. *Insight, Motivation, Discipline*

*M*otivation is the fuel needed to make the decision work—to bring commitment to fruition. Self-discipline (by which I mean neither purposeless self-flagellation nor coercion by outside forces) is the continuing use of resources to reach that goal.

Insight provided by others is useless unless the recipient is desirous of and open to it. Furthermore, that recipient must be motivated sufficiently to discipline himself or herself—to work, to struggle, to harness all his or her resources in accepting, understanding and using that insight in the service of the self. This usually takes humility and a certain neutralization of pride.

On the other hand, motivation—that is, real desire for something—has to come entirely from the self. Salesmen can sell people things they don't want (though I question whether even the most "talented" salesman can sell anyone an item if some kernel of desire is not there deep down inside). By the same token, we can sell ourselves on something we don't really want.

I repeat: The motivation to get what we want through necessary struggle comes from the same place real decisions come from—ourselves. *We* must have the solid desire! *We* must want whatever it is we want—especially if it is connected to real change and growth—enough to expect and accept struggle for it.

Self-discipline is simply self-direction toward a particular goal. And the fact is, *self-discipline directed toward a goal that we are genuinely motivated to achieve is not especially difficult to come by*, if we recognize in advance that struggle is necessary for any worthwhile goal. Where motivation is genuine and self-discipline nevertheless seems to falter (dieters, for instance, are all too familiar with this problem!), the reason is probably not "poor will power" or "a failure of nerve," or any of the other catch phrases we use to punish ourselves and sustain self-hate. Instead, the chances are strong that self-sabotage is taking place. If discipline fails and we are nevertheless convinced that the desire to achieve our goal is genuine, we will be wise to ask whether we may not be unwittingly subverting our healthy aims and desires—that is, whether a decision-killing blockage is at work. We need to explore honestly and courageously what specific thoughts or patterns of behavior may be undermining motivation and discipline and above all ask *why* this seems to be occurring.

This is why insight is such an important and indeed indispensable tool in cultivating decision power. The self-discipline necessary to sustain worthwhile struggle on behalf of a designated choice is attainable! But motivation and discipline can come only from within. They can be aided by support from others (though not if "support" takes the form of sales pitches or coercion). But they must be supported above all by self-knowledge and they must spring from the healthy substance of self, from the desire and struggle for the things we deeply value in life.

18. The Postponement of Gratification

*T*his is an aspect of self-discipline, and an asset no would-be decision-maker can afford to be without.

Someone said, "Nothing without great labor!" Someone should add, "And very little without the willingness to postpone gratification."

Amazingly few people are willing to do this. It is especially difficult for the young and restless. Yet it is one of the most basic of the twenty secrets. Putting off gratification until later in order to attain larger rewards than those immediately available is just about axiomatic to more than minimal success. Choices that ignore this essential are almost never geared for large successes.

I am not advocating unnecessary delays that are really screens for procrastination, resignation, dependency and other forms of pseudodecision. Avoiding commitment by "taking more time"—putting off the course work; never sitting down to write the book; waiting until we "know him/her well enough" to be sure he/she won't reject a request for a date—is about the last way to achieve success and happiness. However, most of us will recognize the difference between a rationalization like "I need more time" and the precept that *solid results require time*—and also effort and struggle.

If we put off doing a thing and find ourselves drifting, going nowhere, we are sabotaging ourselves. If we put off doing it but find that, with struggle and effort, we are slowly progressing toward the desired goal, we can congratulate ourselves on having demonstrated a true willingness to postpone gratification—an enormous asset and an indispensable element in self-realization and success.

Training and development of any kind take time. As the world becomes increasingly complex, increased training and experience are necessary. An inability to wait virtually guarantees small rewards. Rewards are usually geometrically and directly proportional to the ability to endure necessary waiting. There's been no pill invented that confers expertise or experience. To become a surgeon, lawyer, diplomat, business administrator, musician or writer takes time. So do relationships, for that matter—time and, often, effort! During the time that it takes, little or nothing is earned and recognition for work done and energy put out is minimal. These rewards come later. And of course, if the delay results in work that is interesting, gratifying and rewarding in all regards, the postponement of gratification will have led to a situation likely to generate further good decisions and successes.

19. The Value of Struggle

I have written about the value of struggle in many places. I spoke of it just now in regard to other essentials for decision success. It is an essential in itself.

Decision-making *is* healthy struggle.

Our society somehow sees accomplishment without struggle as "the real thing." As a result, I actually encounter many people who suffer in order not to struggle. This is, I suppose, part of the something-for-nothing syndrome that seems to characterize our times—a kind of belief in unreality and magic. This is the result of a self-inflating investment in cleverness, rather than in highly developed proclivities, skills and real work. And I think herein lies the confusion.

Struggle is equated by many with "suffering." Suffering serves self-hate, self-idealization and illusion, and we do in fact suffer when we promote distortions of ourselves. Our *real selves* suffer the consequent aberrations. Worse yet, the need to struggle is often viewed as evidence of being inferior and being singled out for tough times.

But life can be tough for all of us at times. Moreover, we all have to struggle for what we want. This need to struggle doesn't make us inferior. It's just evidence of being human and alive.

I well remember a boyhood friend of mine named Izz, who could pick out tunes on the piano from an astonishingly early age. Our mutual friend and upstairs neighbor, Mort, couldn't do this. However, Izz refused to struggle with learning how to read music or with taking piano lessons. Mort did both. The result: Izz can still pick out tunes. Mort derives and gives much pleasure as a fairly accomplished jazz pianist. In my opinion, Mort, with fewer natural gifts, won the competition hands down. As far as music is concerned, his life is much richer than that of Izz, who never progressed at all.

Struggle serves real self, real growth, real success. Struggle can be difficult, but it is not suffering, in the foregoing sense. Struggle is the mobilization of inner resources. It is concentrating everything in ourselves on the problem at hand. When we struggle, we engage in the process of healthy change and growth. We exercise ourselves and flex all our muscles—physical, intellectual, emotional—in the service of full living.

20. Self-Confidence IV: Knowning and Accepting What It Means to be a Person

Perhaps this is the ultimate "essential" of successful decision-making—acceptance of the human condition in its totality. This includes, of course, having the realistic expectations I advocated earlier in this section. But it means more than just that.

To have true self-esteem—and therefore true self-confidence—we must know and accept what *being human* means.

We must know that we have limits and liabilities, as well as assets; confusions, mixed feelings and conflicts as well as fine insights; anxieties as well as inner peace.

Being human means being healthy and sick; having good and bad moods; having victories and failures. It means that we can communicate easily sometimes and get frustrated to the point of explosion in trying to get an idea across at other times.

Being a person means knowing that it takes struggle and

time to learn anything at all—especially to learn what someone else is feeling.

It means realizing that plenty of seeds within us just won't see the light of day because the time in our lives is limited. It means understanding that there is sorrow and joy, weakness as well as vigor, old age as well as youth. All this is what being human is about.

I guess knowing this really well is maturity. But even more important than maturity is compassion—especially compassion for self. Compassion for self, for our limitations, is an incomparable source of strength and makes self-esteem possible.

Accepting everything there is about being human is pretty hard. But I would define this acceptance as "wisdom." Real wisdom, real acceptance, is extremely rare. It takes genuine humility.

And that, too, is not easy to attain.

VII

Overcoming Indecisiveness!

Some Final Considerations

In the next few pages, I want to leave you with some thoughts about the most common obstacles and problems I see in my practice. They are problems that you can recognize and anticipate and therefore to a certain degree control. If you see yourself in part in any of these, you're already well into the process of making some good decisions in your own life and overcoming indecisiveness in whatever form.

Difficulty in working out relationships is, I believe, the most prevalent and perhaps most important human problem I encounter in my practice. There is no one who escapes the issue, and it usually arises in making the decision to marry, to live together, or to break off an existing relationship that may be based on great mutual attraction or need but still carries substantial conflict. I discuss relationships in detail in my book *One to One*, and I believe that healthy human relationships are the basis for productive living. Knowing who you are and using that self-knowledge to establish and maintain a loving partnership of any kind is usually the basis for self-confidence and thus effective decision-making in other areas of life.

Let me describe briefly some examples of decisons of this kind which may have special conditions attached to them that are sometimes overlooked. I think these will be especially helpful to you in evaluating your own situation.

In deciding to marry or in evaluating an existing relationship, it's important to ask some key questions. Is the marriage based on a shared personal history of some length and richness? Is it based on sufficient common priorities? On personality structures that will enhance each other and not be of a terrible, conflicting nature so as to produce self-hate and mutual hatred? Or is it based on an impulsive pseudodecision and on no substance other than quick mutual infatuation and a passing crush?

In my experience with patients, I have seen every imaginable combination of partners, and while each case is individual and based on a wide variety of circumstances, common patterns do emerge. If two narcissists marry, they will be in a highly competitve situation in which each will want to be the center of attention, getting narcissistic supplies. If two detached people marry, they can be like ships passing in the night. When two self-erasers marry, they may well vie with each other to avoid decisions and responsibility of any kind. On the other hand, expansive people and self-erasing people, all other things being equal, may get along very well together. A detached and an expansive person may get along if their priorities and other criteria are fulfilled at least to some reasonable degree.

Another very common human dilemma is the decision for men and women to divorce or stay together. Again, you must ask: Is the decision to divorce based on impulse or momentary boredom? Is it the result of an inability to struggle for better communication and relatedness? Or could' it be the result of one of the blockages, such as the comparison to imaginary delights that are not present? Or wanting to have it all—freedom and relatedness at the same time? Or is it based on an unfulfilled need for perfectionism?

Conversely, if the decision to divorce is taking place after a considerable struggle indicating that in fact there is a great lack of common priorities and great abrasion from a difficult combination of personalities, it may well be based on true self-knowledge and not be misguided. Chances are excellent that the individuals involved made a pseudodecision in the first place based on inadequate investigation into who each of them was at the time of the marriage and how they related together. And chances are excellent that they had insufficient quality time together. In fact, the two most common reasons for divorce I have found in my patients are an initial ignorance of their own and each other's priorities and an unwillingness to postpone gratification, in favor of instant communication.

Another frequent and difficult decision comes in choosing whether or not to have a child or, when childbirth is impossible or for some reason not preferred, in choosing to adopt. If the choice is made out of boredom or an attempt to alleviate it, chances are it's a pseudodecision. Likewise, if a couple uses this as a remedy to help a failing marriage—a tragically common occurrence—that's often a pseudodecision. A lack of awareness of one's own ability or inability to take on enormous responsibility and make any enormous emotional investment can make for poor choices and pseudodecisions as well. However, if the desire to have a child is based on the healthy wish for family existence and all that it implies—including the activation of our need for caring and getting the satisfaction derived from helping another human being realize his or her potential—it's a decision likely to be based on self-knowledge. Again, simply knowing one's motives and understanding the choice mean real decision-making.

Smoking, overdrinking and overeating are three very common human tendencies that I encounter over and over in my practice and that I group together because, more often than not, they are motivated by the same urges, and the inability to overcome them can be found in the same blockages. The desire to overcome a problem of this sort may be aided by vanity and even by narcissism, ironically. But the decision to overcome an addiction to food or alcohol or cigarettes will not be sustained unless real confrontation has taken place, and the immediate desire for the alleviation of anxiety and for pleasure is overcome. Then the desire for a healthier, longer life can be made active.

I believe that the greatest failure of organizations that attempt to aid people in the decision to give up any addiction—particularly the addiction to overeating—is the fact that they ignore the gratification that comes from eating or smoking or drinking. In essence, gratification of this kind comes from the blockage we have talked about—the avoidance of conflict. What I am really saying here is that the conflict between immediate gratification from the addictive substance and the desire for health must be confronted fully and consciously before a decision for sustained health can be made on a meaningful and effective level. You have to know what you're giving up in order to give it up effectively, and as I've said, that means recognizing the conflict. It should be pointed out, too, that addiction itself is a form of resignation, which works hand in hand with avoidance of conflict. I suggest strongly that if you suffer from overeating or the others, familiarizing yourself with these blockages will be a big help.

Overcoming Indecisiveness!

*S*uccess in any area leading to achievements that come from decisions based on free choice—choices reflecting our selves and our own priorities and values—is a good bet for happiness. Achievements consistent with who we really are make a fertile ground for happiness.

Conversely, achievement that comes purely from compulsive aggression (the need to have power or mastery over others), from conformist obedience to cultural or social dictates, or from a need for vindictive triumphs—such as revenge—leaves a hole, a chronic yearning and a sense of impoverishment, regardless of the apparent magnitude of the achievement. Nor do I believe that real achievement, much less happiness, lies in the possession of status symbols or creature comforts: creature comforts used only to show off become burdensome addictions (though in the presence of genuine self-esteem they can be fun).

Finally, "happiness" in this limited human world of ours

can never mean permanent euphoria, or eternal freedom from further struggle, further decision. But within the limitations of human reality, maximum self-realization *is* an attainable goal—through achievements consistent with reality and with who we really are.

Having decision power, and the extraordinary inner freedom that it bestows, makes this kind of happiness possible.

The acceptance of struggle contributes enormously both to decision power and to inner freedom. And, perhaps more than anything else, so does the acceptance and knowledge of self.

Let me leave you with these thoughts:

1. You can be at least as happy with decision success as without it. You can also spend at least as much time and energy avoiding decision power as you are likely to spend in acquiring it.

2. Overcoming indecisiveness and decision success does not happen (nor does happiness) without high motivation. You must want it enough to struggle and to work at it.

3. Decision ownership is ownership of self—thoughts, feelings, values.

4. Self-esteem helps decision power enormously. Those who have learned self-esteem in childhood are blessed. None of us must fail to give it to ourselves wherever possible.

5. We must have compassion for self and loyalty to self—no matter what. This enhances self-esteem and self-confidence.

6. Self-hate destroys self-esteem. When self-hate is expressed in the form of self-sabotage and blockages to decision success, it must be neutralized and destroyed, wherever it is recognized, with self-knowledge, compassion and insight.

7. Real decision-making is *in and of, itself* one of the most valuable aids to self-knowledge, the destruction of self-hate and increased self-esteem. Self-knowledge of the best kind is aided by knowing our own human assets.

8. In knowing our priorities, we learn to know ourselves. Through the very process of designating a free, committed choice, we strengthen self and muster our resources in the service of healthy growth and change.

9. We must have hope and optimism about our own decisions! There are inevitable frustrations and disappointments to get through. Hope and motivation are quintessential elements in transcending the bumps along the road to the designated goal.

10. Finally, we must have hope for ourselves! We almost always participate in our own prophecies about ourselves. With hope, self-compassion and self-knowledge, we turn ourselves in the direction of decision, success and happiness.

Working at decision-making means taking full advantage of the human prerogative. We alone as a species have the potential of choice and decision—of options beyond instinctual, biological dictates. This is real freedom. This is real power. Making decisions gives us the freedom to exert power in living our own lives.

Index